500 Best Genealogy & Family History Tips

2023 Edition

by Thomas MacEntee

500 Best Genealogy and Family History Tips.
Copyright © 2023 by Thomas MacEntee. Print edition.

All rights reserved. No part of this book can be reproduced in any form without permission in writing from the author. Reviewers may quote brief passages in reviews.

Disclaimer and FTC Notice

No part of this publication may be reproduced or transmitted in any form or by any means, mechanical or electronic, including photocopying or recording, or by any information storage and retrieval system, or transmitted by email without permission in writing from the publisher.

While all attempts have been made to verify the information provided in this publication, neither the author nor the publisher assumes any responsibility for errors, omissions, or contrary interpretations of the subject matter herein.

Neither the author nor the publisher assumes any responsibility or liability whatsoever on behalf of the purchaser or reader of these materials.

From time to time, I will use affiliate links in my books and guides. What does this mean? Well, if you click on the link and make a purchase, I get a small sales commission. This is part of my business strategy. I'm not selling my opinion or endorsement by using these links; when I use affiliate links, it means I believe in the product and have built up a relationship with the vendor. You should always do your own research on any product you purchase online.

Table of Contents

Introduction 7
Genealogy Rules to Live By 8
Books 12
    Google Books 12
    Free Digital Libraries You May Not Know 13
    Library Organizing Apps and Websites 15
    WorldCat 15
    Family History Books at FamilySearch 15
City and Business Directories 16
    Resources for City and Business Directories 18
Data Backup 20
    Cloud Storage Sites 21
    Online Backup Methods 22
    Photo Storage 23
    Things You Didn't Know You Could or Should Back Up 23
    Data Backup Tips and Tricks 24
DropBox 25
    Best DropBox Features 26
    DropBox Tips and Tricks 27
Education 29
    Crafting a Genealogy Education Plan 29
    Converting Acquired Knowledge into Action 30
    Keep On Learning: Online and Offline Resources 31
Facebook 33
    How Genealogists Use Facebook 34
    Facebook Best Practices 35

Frugal Genealogy – FREE Stuff! 36
Getting Organized & Information Overload 43
Giving Back 46
Google..48
    Google Alerts 48
    Google Books 49
    Google Drive...49
    Google Forms 50
    Google Images 50
    Google Newspapers 50
    Google Search Tricks 51
    Google Translate 51
Mapping Your Genealogy...52
    Types of Maps 52
    Genealogical Uses for Maps 54
    Online and Offline Historic Map Resources..........55
Photos 56
    Metadata 56
    Photo Gifts 57
    Scanning Photos...58
Pinning Your Family History 60
    What to Pin? 62
    Pinning Sites You Should Know 62
Playing Nice in the Genealogy Sandbox 64
    Getting What You Need From Family Members ...64
    How to Deal with Librarians, Archivists, and Others 66
    Correcting Information in a Collaborative Environment.........69
    Giving and Receiving Proper Credit 69
    The Do's and Don'ts of Collaborating and Sharing 71
    Genealogy Conflict Resolution 71

Potpourri – What They Never Tell You about Genealogy 73
Black Sheep and the Dark Side of Genealogy 73
Collateral and Cluster Searching 73
Finding the Living... 74
Name Variations 75

Preserving Family History 76
Communication and Scheduling 77
Recording Devices and Platforms 78
Interview Questions and Prompts.. 78
Sharing Methods and Platforms 79
Tips and Tricks for Interviewing Family Members 79
Follow Up Materials 82
Organizing and Producing Your Family's Story..................... 82
Cleaning or Consolidating a Home 83
Converting Old Media 85
After You're Gone 86

Research Logs and Methodology............................... 88

Self-Publishing 90

Smarter Search Strategies for Genealogy................. 93
Smarter Searching Resources 95

Social Media.. 97
Benefits of Social Networking for Genealogists 98
The Do's and Don'ts of Social Networking 99

Staying Safe Online.. 101
Terms of Service and Settings 102
Privacy 103
Friends and Followers 104
Games and Applications.. 106
Pitfalls and Stuff to Avoid... 106

Take Action	108
Tech Grab Bag	**109**
Travel Tips	**112**
A Genealogist's Packing List	112
How to Handle Emergencies	112
Leverage Loyalty Programs	114
Sponsored Research Trips	114
Set Up Alerts for Deals and Discounts	114
Travel Apps and Websites	115
Time To Go Pro?	**118**
Starting a Genealogy Business	**120**
Set Goals and Create a Business Plan	121
Read, Write and THINK	121
Finances and Taxes	122
Legal Issues	122
Marketing	123
Networking and Professional Development	123
Marketing and Selling	124
Analytics	124
The Future of Genealogy	**125**
About the Author – Thomas MacEntee	**131**
Ways to Connect with Thomas MacEntee	**133**
FREE Genealogy Cheat Sheets	**134**

Introduction

500 Best Genealogy & Family History Tips is best described as a "brain dump" of me, Thomas MacEntee, and my years of knowledge about genealogy and family history. Basically, what I've done is to extract my favorite tips and tricks from over 85 presentations, 40 cheat sheets, 10 books and numerous articles. In addition, I've reviewed the social media posts and conversations from Facebook, Twitter, and other platforms for issues important to today's genealogists.

What will you find in this "best tips" guide? Everything from practical ways to use Google, advice on protecting your privacy online, information about secret or little known resources for genealogy research, and more. The best way to use this guide is to browse the Table of Contents to find a topic of interest. Also simply search the book when trying to find a solution to a problem, such as how to cite a source or locate an app to generate bibliographic information.

I hope you enjoy ***500 Best Genealogy & Family History Tips*** and put it to good use in the coming year.

500 Best Genealogy & Family History Tips covers a wide range of topics including:

- genealogy research methodology and strategy
- how to use websites such as Google and Internet Archive to find your ancestors
- realizing the power of Facebook, Instagram, and other social media platforms for genealogy
- preserving family photos and stories
- staying safe using social media
- how to secure your genealogy data on your computer and in the cloud

and more!

Genealogy Rules to Live By

If you know me, I'm not a very "rules oriented" guy; for me rules are meant to be broken. These rules are more like "guideposts" along my genealogy journey. They keep me focused and they keep me grounded. When I'm stressed over a genealogy research project or I'm having trouble communicating a concept to others, I review this simple list that is posted on my office wall.

1. **There is no Easy Button in genealogy.** You will work hard to find your ancestors. Genealogy will require more than passion; it will require skills, smarts, and dedication. Don't believe the hype of instant hints, smart matches, and shaky leaves. If it were that easy, the journey of discovering our roots would have little or no meaning.

2. **Research from a place of "I Don't Know."** Your genealogy research will likely run counter to your cherished family stories. It will upend your preconceived notions about certain events and people. It will change the way you think about your ancestors. This can only happen if you research with an open mind and take off the blinders.

3. **Track Your Work and Cite Your Sources.** When I started out in genealogy, I'll admit I was a name collector and would "dump" almost any name into my database. Years later, I am crossing out entire branches of a tree that never really should have been "grafted" on to mine. Use a research log, track your work, cite your sources, and analyze data <u>before</u> it is entered into any software or online family tree program.

4. **Ask for help.** The genealogy community is populated with people of all skill levels and areas of expertise, most of whom want to assist others. There are no stupid questions; we all started as beginners. There is no right way to ask. Post a query on Facebook or ask a question during a webinar or email your favorite genealogy rock star.

5. **You can't edit a blank page.** Which means you have to <u>start</u> in order to have something to work with. That project you keep putting off, like publishing your family history, won't complete itself. Commit yourself to move from "obsession" to "reality." Remember: *A year from now, you'll wish you had started today.*

6. **Work and think like your ancestors.** While I'm not sure about your ancestors, mine were resourceful and developed tools and skills to get what they wanted. They were not "educated" *per se*, but they had "street smarts" and knew where to go so they could learn new things. Also have a plan; my ancestors didn't just wake up one day and on a whim decided to come to America and make a better life. They had a plan, they had a network of people to help them, and they made it happen.

7. **You do not own your ancestors.** Researching your roots can create emotional connections to not only your ancestors but to the actual research itself. Many become "possessive" of their ancestors and fail to realize that a 3rd great-grandparent is likely the ancestor of hundreds of others. You can't take your research or your ancestor with you when you die; take time to share your research and be open to differences in information and research when collaborating with others.

8. **Be nice. The genealogy community is a small place.** While there are millions of people searching for ancestors, genealogists worldwide have developed a community with relatively few degrees of separation. Whether it is online in a Facebook group or in-person at genealogy conference, it is likely you'll already know someone. Being "genealogy nice" is not fake; the connections with other researchers tend to be deep and genuine. We know that all of our roots are interlocked, and a genealogist can't always go it alone.

9. **Give and be abundant.** Exchange information freely with other researchers; don't hold data "close" to you or exchange it in lieu of something else. Most genealogists who have heard me speak know my story of abundance: don't let your hand keep a tight grip on information. Let it go. Once your hand is free, it can be open and ready to receive the next good thing coming your way.

Books

Throughout history, books have been the mainstay of genealogical research. Here are some tips on getting the most out of books, whether they are in print or digital.

Google Books

A resource of over 40 million books in digital format, **Google Book**s (https://books.google.com) contains many volumes of interest to genealogists.

10. Use **Advanced Search** to limit your search to only free books (Full View) (https://books.google.com/advanced_book_search)

11. Make sure you look at **Preview** and **Snippet View** results in a Google Book search! Sometimes the page you need with important genealogy information will be available!

12. All issues of **Ancestry Magazine**, which ceased publication in 2010, are available for free on Google Books (https://genealogybargains.com/googlebooks-ancestrymag).

13. Use the **Get the book** function to find the library nearest your location that has the book available for use.

14. Create a virtual bookshelf and "save" your favorite books on Google Books. Sign in with a Google account, then click **My Library** in Google Books.

15. Have a print version of a book delivered to your local library via WorldCat (https://www.worldcat.org/) by clicking **Get the Book** and scroll down to the **Borrow** section.

Free Digital Libraries You May Not Know

It isn't all about Google Books! There are many FREE online sites where you can access books, magazines and even census microfilms as well as recorded interviews.

16. **250+ Killer Digital Libraries and Archives** (https://www.oedb.org/ilibrarian/250-plus-killer-digital-libraries-and-archives/)

17. **Alex Catalogue of Electronic Texts** (http://infomotions.com/alex/)

18. **Bartleby.com** (https://www.bartleby.com/)

19. **British History Online** (https://www.british-history.ac.uk/)

20. **CARLI Digital Collections** (https://collections.carli.illinois.edu/)

21. **Europeana** (https://www.europeana.eu/en)

22. **Hathi Trust** (https://www.hathitrust.org/)
23. **Internet Archive** (https://archive.org/details/books)
24. **Internet Public Library** (https://www.ipl.org/)
25. **Library of Congress Digital Collections** (https://www.loc.gov/collections/)
26. **Harvard Digital Collections** (https://library.harvard.edu/digital-collections)
27. **Open Library** (https://openlibrary.org/)
28. **Project Gutenberg** (https://www.gutenberg.org).
29. **Smithsonian Digital Library Online** (https://library.si.edu/digital-library)
30. **The European Library** (https://www.theeuropeanlibrary.org/)
31. **The Online Books Page** (https://onlinebooks.library.upenn.edu/)
32. **Trove** (National Library of Australia) (https://trove.nla.gov.au/)

Library Organizing Apps and Websites

Do you have a collection of genealogy and family history books that you want to inventory and keep organized? These apps and websites make it easy!

33. **BookLikes** (https://booklikes.com/)

34. **GoodReads** (https://www.goodreads.com)

35. **libib** (https://www.libib.com/)

36. **Library Thing** (https://www.librarything.com/)

37. **Shelfari** (https://www.shelfari.com/)

WorldCat

38. Check out **WorldCat** (https://www.worldcat.org) to locate books that can be sent to your local library for a small fee. WorldCat connects you with over 10,000 libraries around the world.

Family History Books at FamilySearch

39. FamilySearch has consolidated the digital holdings of several libraries into one site at **Family Search Digital Library** (https://www.familysearch.org/library/books/). The collection includes over 150,000 genealogy and family history publications from the archives of some of the most important family history libraries in the world.

City and Business Directories

R. L. POLK & CO.'S
Flint City Directory
...1918...

ABBREVIATIONS

adv.	advertisement	n e cor	northeast corner
agt.	agent	nr.	near
assn.	association	n w cor	northwest corner
asst.	assistant	opp.	opposite
av.	avenue	opr.	operator
bet.	between	phys.	physician
bldg.	building	pres.	president
blksmith.	blacksmith	propr.	proprietor
bkpr.	bookkeeper	publr.	publisher
carp.	carpenter	r	rear
cash.	cashier	res.	residence
clk.	clerk	Rev.	Reverend
c.	colored	rd.	road
cond.	conductor	rms.	rooms
cor.	corner	s.	south, or south of
e.	east, or east of	s e cor	southeast corner
e s	east side	sec.	secretary
h.	home	s s	south side
lab.	laborer	stenog.	stenographer
mach.	machinist	supt.	superintendent
mkr.	maker	tchr.	teacher
mnfr.	manufacturer	treas	treasurer
mngr.	manager	whol.	wholesale
mnfg.	manufacturing	w.	west, or west of
mtrmn.	motormen	w s.	west side
n.	north, or north of	wks.	works

ALPHABETICAL LIST OF NAMES

Abair Leon H (Jeanette C), mgr Newark Shoe Stores Co, bds 1222 Lyon
Abar Charles, paperhgr, bds 408 W 2d av
Abbenante A Joseph, director Strand Theatre, res s end S Saginaw

Prior to the invention of the telephone and the telephone book, most cities and even small towns had a directory listing information on their inhabitants. Even after the telephone became popular, and up through the 1920s and 1930s, many towns continued to publish these directories. City and business directories are filled with clues to help you break down brick walls and better understand your ancestors.

40. **Search last name only.** The formatting for city directories is different than most records and using the "first name last name" search will prove frustrating.

41. **Beware of address changes.** Many cities "reconfigured" their address schema or street grid at some point. This usually occurred as cities grew. The address listed in a directory in 1908 may not correspond to the current address.

42. **Browse images by surname.** Make sure you review the entire list of people with the same surname as your ancestor. Check the names against your family tree and you may be able to fill in some gaps.

43. **Understand the abbreviations.** While most abbreviations were standardized across directories ("w" or "wd" for widow, "bd" for "boarder"), check the front or back of the directory for a list of abbreviations.

44. **What is the date of the directory?** Keep in mind that information listed in a directory was often collected up to one year PRIOR to the date on the cover. A 1908 directory could show where your ancestor lived in 1907. Check the front/back pages of the directory to see how information was collected.

45. **Can't find a directory for your town?** Locate the nearest larger town or city and check that directory. Often you will find that smaller villages and hamlets are included in the directories of larger cities.

46. **Don't ignore the table of contents!** You would be surprised at what is contained in a directory by consulting the "TOC." Often there will be street names, lists of churches, fraternal and charitable organizations, and more.

47. **Use Google Maps Street View.** Once you've determined an address, check out the current view on Google Maps Street View and see if the building still exists.

48. **Search by address.** Once you have located an ancestor at a specific address, use that address to search other directories in the same town or city.

49. **Create timelines.** Track your ancestor over time once you've collected information over the course of several years in a city directory.

Resources for City and Business Directories

50. **Ancestry – City and Area Directories**
    https://www.ancestry.com/search/categories/dir_city/

51. **Ancestry – US City Directories 1822-1995**
    https://search.ancestry.com/search/db.aspx?dbid=2469

52. **City Directory Abbreviations – GenealogyInTime Magazine**
    http://www.genealogyintime.com/dictionaries/city-directory-abbreviations.html

53. **Don's List**
    http://www.donslist.net/PGHLookups/Dir1Win.shtml

54. **Fold3 – City Directories, 1728 -1926**
    https://go.fold3.com/citydirectories

55. **Digital Public Library of America – Directories**
    https://dp.la/search?q=city%20directories

56. **Google Books**
    https://books.google.com/

57. **Hathi Trust**
    https://www.hathitrust.org/

58. **Internet Archive – Directories**
    https://archive.org/search.php?query=directory

59. **Library of Congress – City Directories Online**
    https://www.loc.gov/search/?in=&q=city+directory&new=true

60. **MyHeritage City Directories**
    https://www.myheritage.com/research/collection-10705/us-city-directories

61. **Online Historical Directories**
    https://sites.google.com/site/onlinedirectorysite/Home/

62. **The Newberry Library – City Directories**
    https://newberry.org/city-directories

63. **United States Directories** – FamilySearch Wiki
    https://www.familysearch.org/wiki/en/United_States_Directories

64. **Zillow - Real Estate Listings**
    https://www.zillow.com

Data Backup

Be honest with yourself right now: when was the last time you backed up your genealogy data? Take this test: if you didn't have your computer or laptop or even mobile phone right now, what data would you lose? How long would it take you to reconstruct it? Where would you go to get information? Your genealogy research data is an investment reflecting the time and effort you've spent tracing your roots. Like any other investment, your genealogy data should be safe and secure for future use.

Here are some tips on ensuring your data is secure!

65. **Make a Data Backup Plan**. Institute the 3-2-1 Backup Plan for backing up data: 3 backups, 2 different media, and 1 backup offsite. This means you can't just rely on one backup. And you should not use the same media (USB flash drive, external hard drive, etc.) for each of those backups. And finally, make sure at least one backup is located AWAY from your computer … either a USB flash drive in a safety deposit box, or a backup in "the cloud."

66. **Never Lose a USB Flash Drive Again!** Ever leave a USB flash drive in a computer at a research library? There are two simple tricks to improve your odds of having your flash drive returned: 1) place a return address label on the outside with your name and email address and 2) create a text file (ends in .txt) named **_Reward If Found** and list your name, email address and other contact information. Most library staff will do a simple check in the main directory of a lost flash drive in order to reunite it with its owner!

67. **Get an External Hard Drive**. Don't rely solely on a cloud based backup solution such as Dropbox, Carbonite, or others; make sure you have a portable external hard drive installed on your computer. The current trend is to use portable Solid State Drives which are as low as $60 USD for a 1TB capacity drive.

Cloud Storage Sites

Most cloud storage sites offer some form of free storage, and all will synchronize your files so they can be accessed from all your devices.

68. **Box**: Offers 10GB of free synchronized storage (https://www.box.com/).

69. **Dropbox**: Automatic synching of files of any size or type to different computers. Includes mobile option and file sharing. Free option allows up to 2 GB of storage (https://www.dropbox.com).

70. **Google Drive**: Formerly Google Docs, offers file storage and automatic synching with a free option of up to 15 GB of storage (https://drive.google.com).

71. **iDrive**: Offers continuous universal backup of PCs, Macs, iPhones, iPads, and Android devices. Free option allows up to 5GB of storage (https://www.idrive.com/).

72. **OneDrive**: Microsoft's version of online storage and backup. Requires a Windows Live ID and offers RSS feeds. Free version is 7 GB (https://www.microsoft.com/en-us/microsoft-365/onedrive/online-cloud-storage).

Online Backup Methods

Online backup programs take the hassle out of backing up your data with no hardware to buy. You pay a monthly or yearly fee, and they take care of the rest!

73. **Backblaze**: Backs up everything on your personal computer except for the operating system, applications, and temporary files. Includes PC and Mac as well as external drives for $50 per year (https://www.backblaze.com/).

74. **Carbonite**: Backup personal data with no limit on storage space. Plans start at $59 per computer per year (https://www.carbonite.com).

Photo Storage

75. **Dropbox Photos**. Use the **Dropbox Photos** feature to store, view and share photos (https://www.dropbox.com/features/photos).

76. **Flickr**. Yahoo offers 1TB of free photo storage via **Flickr** (https://www.flickr.com). Options include the ability to edit and share photos with others.

77. **Google Photos**. Formerly Picasa, Google Photos (https://photos.google.com/) offers up to 15GB of free photo storage (shared with your Google Drive and Gmail accounts).

Things You Didn't Know You Could or Should Back Up

Have you considered these areas of data to back up?

78. **Internet Favorites and Bookmarks**. Usually stored under your c:\Documents and Settings folder but they may also be stored in your Internet browser program file directory if you are using a browser such as Google Chrome or Firefox.

79. **Emails**. Don't forget those emails from distant relatives or other researchers. Download in a non-proprietary format (html, txt, etc.) for safekeeping.

80. **Facebook**: Download a copy of all your Facebook data in XML format (https://www.facebook.com/help/212802592074644).

81. **Twitter**: Go to **Settings** (https://twitter.com/settings/account), scroll down and click **Download an archive of your data**.

Data Backup Tips and Tricks

82. **Make sure you identify all your data.** Remember that genealogy data can hide in the weirdest places on your computer. Think beyond genealogy software and include favorites, bookmarks, emails, and photos.

83. **Keep a regular schedule.** Backing up on a regular basis—not just when you remember to do it—is the key to successfully ensuring your data is available in case of a mishap. Whether it is a sticky note on the wall in your office, an automated reminder in your email or online calendar, set up a schedule.

84. **Automate as much as possible.** If you don't currently think much about data backups, then select an automated process that does all the thinking for you! Look for online backups such as Carbonite, Dropbox or Mozy. Or use an external hard drive with software that will perform a backup on a regular basis.

85. **Test your backups.** All your planning and work aren't worth anything if you aren't capturing all your data during backups or your backup can't restore data properly. Don't wait until Kitty knocks that glass of water all over your laptop to find out that your backup process stopped working six months ago. Periodically test your backups. Also realize that CDs and DVDs can degrade over time.

86. **Use current technology.** Data backups should be in a format that can be used in the future. If a technology starts to fade—like 5 1/4" floppy drives—make sure you upgrade your backup method.

DropBox

Dropbox is an online data repository available to the public using the "freemium" concept. This means a basic service – in the case of Dropbox, the maximum storage space is 2GB – is provided for free in hopes that you, the consumer, will value it so much that you'll upgrade to the paid version of the program.

87. **Getting Started**. 1) Go to https://www.dropbox.com and in the upper left-hand corner, click **Log In**. 2) Click **Create an account**. 3) Download and Install the **Dropbox Application**. 4) Start **adding data** to the Dropbox folder.

88. **Understand How the Sync Feature Works**. Synchronizing files or "synching" is easy to understand if you visualize having several different computers or devices all with Dropbox installed:

Desktop Computer

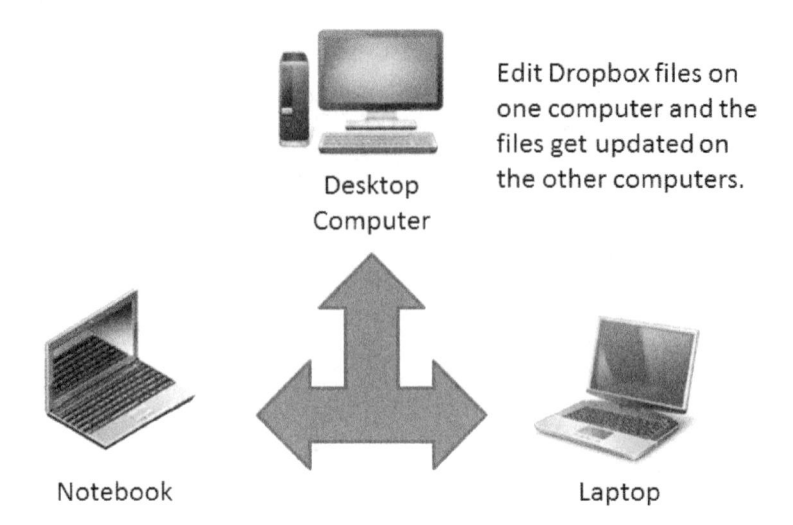

Edit Dropbox files on one computer and the files get updated on the other computers.

Notebook

Laptop

You will see a status notification in your Taskbar area in the lower right of your computer screen when changes are made to Dropbox files from any of the locations. Even if one of these computers is turned off, the files will be updated once it is powered on and connected to the Internet.

Best DropBox Features

89. **Share Dropbox Folders and Files with Others.** Dropbox allows you to "invite" others to access a common data folder in Dropbox. At the Dropbox website, click the **Share** button.

90. **Dropbox Photos**. Use the **Dropbox Photos** feature to store, view and share photos (https://www.dropbox.com/features/photos).

91. **Upload Using the Dropbox Folder Sync Addon.** Use a menu that appears when you "right click" over a folder with the mouse. See **Dropbox Folder Sync Addon** (https://satyadeepk.in/dropbox-folder-sync/).

92. **Install the Mobile App**. You can access your Dropbox files from a smart device by installing the Dropbox app. Visit the Apple store (https://www.apple.com/store) or Google Play store (https://play.google.com/store/) depending upon your device operating system.

93. **Restore Deleted Files**. One incredible and sometimes "lifesaving" feature of Dropbox is the ability to restore items that have been deleted. This can come in handy especially if a member of a shared folder has removed a document or overwritten data by accident. On the Dropbox website, on the **Files** tab, click **Show deleted files**. Deleted files will appear in a lighter text than other files. Click the drop-down menu on the right side of the file and select **Undelete**. The file will be restored.

94. **Check Out Other Dropbox Apps**. New apps can be found at **Dropbox Apps Center** (https://www.dropbox.com/apps).

DropBox Tips and Tricks

95. **Check the Events Tab**. On the Dropbox website, the **Events** tab allows you to track activity related to your Dropbox files. Dropbox retains files history for the past 30 days.

96. **How Much Free Space Do You Have Left?** At the Dropbox website, click on **Account** in the upper left corner to manage your Dropbox account. On the **Account Info** tab, you can see how much space you have used so far.

97. **Where Do You Have Dropbox Installed?** At the Dropbox website, click on **Account** in the upper left corner to manage your Dropbox account. On the **My Computers** tab, you can see the names of the computers and "unlink" these computers.

98. **Download Free or Cheap E-books on Dropbox.** Search for free or low-cost e-books about Dropbox on Amazon (https://genealogybargains.com/amazon-dropbox); also remember to save the link as a bookmark or favorite and check for new books periodically!

99. **Need More Dropbox Help?** Check out *The Ultimate Unofficial Dropbox Guide* (https://genealogybargains.com/amazon-unofficial-dropbox).

Education

Genealogy is a continual learning journey: in order to make progress in research, we need to understand methodologies, record sets and more. The genealogy community offers a variety of free and fee sources of solid education.

Crafting a Genealogy Education Plan

100. **Plan Document**. Don't get hung up on whether to keep you plan on paper, a spreadsheet, etc. The important thing is to just have a plan. Use a format that works for you.

101. **What's your learning style?** Some of us like webinars or can't afford to travel to large conferences; others prefer "in person" learning opportunities. Some like short one-hour sessions; others prefer week long genealogy institutes. Make notes on how you like to learn then match your options to your preferences.

102. **Options**. Use some of the resources below or search for genealogy education on the Internet. Just like collecting negative evidence in genealogy research, on your planning document also include those options you won't use and state <u>why</u> you won't use them.

103. **Get recommendations**. Thanks to social media, it is easy to ask for opinions from other genealogists and family historians as to what educational offerings they feel are successful.

104. **Be willing to try something new**. You never know when something will just "click" . . . you've had this happen during a genealogy class or presentation, right? So, try to go outside your comfort zone when selecting an option.

Converting Acquired Knowledge into Action

105. **Set up an exploration day**. Schedule time each week, a block of one or two hours, and select a topic to explore. Get out those handouts or look at your education plan. Example: if you attended a class on using mortality schedules, locate sites where you can access the schedules, understand the layout of information and search to see if any of your ancestors are listed.

106. **Take notes**. One of the best ways to absorb information is to take notes during a presentation. An even better method is to go to those notes as soon as you can and type them up and add them to your education plan. Your recall is better right after the class, and typing up the notes will reinforce the learning.

107. Tell others. If you have a blog, website, or you have access to Facebook, post a short overview of a recent genealogy class and what you learned. It's always nice to hear from other genealogists as to other educational offerings, who presented the topic, what was covered, etc.

Keep On Learning: Online and Offline Resources

108. FamilySearch Research Wiki. Over 80,000 articles covering genealogy, the FamilySearch Research Wiki (https://www.familysearch.org/en/wiki/Main_Page) offers a Wikipedia-like experience for genealogists. Use the wiki to learn more about record sets as well as specific geographical locations.

109. Genealogy Conferences. Looking for an upcoming genealogy event? **Conference Keepers** (https://conferencekeeper.org/) lists genealogy conferences and events all over the world.

110. Genealogy Cruises. If you have never considered taking a cruise and adding genealogy to the mix, you do not know what you are missing! Several genealogy software vendors offer yearly cruises to destinations domestic and international. Usually there are 300+ genealogists in the group on board a larger ship with up to 3,000 people. The group attends genealogy classes while the ship is at sea, and it is just like being at a genealogy conference. In addition, there are organized social activities, the chance to share meals with other family historians and more.

111. Genealogy Tip Jar. Several genealogists have added resources to a group board entitled **Genealogy Tip Jar** (https://www.pinterest.com/genealogybargains/genealogy-tip-jar/) on Pinterest. See if you can't find some new tips and tricks over there!

112. **Twitter Chats**. If you are a fan of Twitter and its micro-blogging functions, consider participating in **GenChat** (https://www.genchatgenealogy.com/).

113. **Have you been to a genealogy institute?** Consider immersing yourself for a week or a weekend in a genealogy-focused environment with other family historians. Check out **Salt Lake Institute of Genealogy** (https://slig.ugagenealogy.org/index.php), **Genealogy Research Institute of Pittsburgh** (https://www.gripitt.org/), **Institute of Genealogy and Historical Research** (https://ighr.gagensociety.org/) and even the new **Virtual Institute of Genealogical Research** (https://www.vigrgenealogy.com/).

Facebook

Facebook is a web-based social media program that allows you to interact with friends and family. You can share photos, discussions, videos, movies and even genealogy research data. While Facebook may be thought of as being the domain of the young (perhaps because of its creator and CEO) recent data shows that the Silver Surfers now rule Facebook!

114. **Create a Facebook Account**. The easiest way to get started is to download *The Facebook Guide Book* (https://mashable.com/category/facebook).

115. **"Skip" Over Initial Steps**. When setting up a Facebook account, use the Skip link in the lower right. DO NOT let Facebook access your email to let others know you are on Facebook. DO NOT answer Facebook's questions about where you went to school etc. You can complete this information later once your account is set up!

How Genealogists Use Facebook

116. **Locate long-lost relatives.** Due to its powerful search feature, Facebook is the perfect place for locating long-lost relatives or even cousins you never knew about! Of course, it is easier when you search for more unusual surnames, but many genealogists have been able to locate far-flung family members. The added bonus comes when they are also working on genealogy research!

117. **Find other genealogists.** Many researchers on Facebook are only too happy to meet and interact with others also interested in family history. You would also be surprised who is researching some of the same ancestral lines!

118. **Ask a question.** Post a question on your News Feed or in a group. Ask for help with research resources or see if other genealogists can do a lookup for you.

119. **Join "virtual" genealogy societies and groups.** Organizations focused and various aspects of genealogy abound on Facebook. You can become a fan on their Fan Page and follow the latest news. And all for free!

120. **Keep up on the latest genealogy industry news.** All the big players - Ancestry, footnote, World Vital Records, NGS, APG - they are all on Facebook in some form or another. Become a friend or a fan and you have instant access to what is going on in the family history world.

Facebook Best Practices

121. Remember Your Audience! Watch what you say on Facebook especially when co-workers or family members are your Facebook friends. They will have access to almost every status update or note you publish including the one about you kissing your cousin Don or playing hooky from work last week!

122. Do not use email links - go to Facebook. If you receive an email purporting to be from Facebook to confirm a new friend or to join a group, delete it and go to your Facebook homepage. You will receive notification on your homepage of any invitations, confirmations, and other items.

123. Friend or foe? Carefully monitor your friend requests and determine if you actually know the person. Do not be afraid to send a message asking how they know you especially if there is no indication of mutual friends.

124. Beware of quizzes! Although they look like fun and a neat way to learn more about your friends, a quiz is often a means of getting you to disclose info that can be used in identity theft purposes. Do not provide data such as your mother's maiden name, where you went to school, the name of your first pet - these are all questions that online banking and other websites use to verify your identity.

125. Understand how Facebook privacy features work. Privacy issues are not restricted only to Facebook; it is incumbent upon you, the user, to read and understand the Terms of Service for every website where you create a profile and post personal information. Once your Facebook account is created you should go to https://www.facebook.com/settings?tab=privacy. Set all your items to **Friends Only**.

Frugal Genealogy – FREE Stuff!

Researching your family history can be fun, but like many hobbies, it can turn into an obsession, and an expensive one at that. There are many ways to save money while you pursue the "hunt" for your roots: some are just common sense while others are, quite frankly, ingenious. Also keep in mind that it doesn't pay to be so focused on "frugal" that in the long run you either lose money or that genealogy is no longer "fun."

126. **Why Genealogy Isn't Free**. It isn't easy to consolidate the "why aren't genealogy records free?" argument into a short paragraph, but here goes: Yes many vital records and other records are public domain or owned by federal and state governments. But it takes money to scan and digitize these items and then not only host the images on a website but also index them in such a way that you can find what you need. In addition, some vendors like Ancestry.com employ proprietary methods of making images easier to use and read – these too cost money to develop. Most of the records are free, if

you are willing to travel to the closest NARA location or a state archive, then search through the items.

127. **Holidays Mean Freebies**. If you don't have a membership to a subscription site like Ancestry.com or MyHeritage, look for "free days" around specific holidays. Very often the week before Memorial Day or Veterans Day will allow you to access military records. Labor Day offers occupational records for free. Sign up for a site's e-mail alerts to stay on top of the latest offers.

128. **Cycle On and Cycle Off**. A common technique many genealogists use to save money is to purchase a short-term membership on a research site like Ancestry.com. Instead of signing up and paying for a year, get a three or six month membership. Once the membership has expired, take a break, and then use other websites for research. Maintain a research log "wish list" of records you want to access or find, and then sign up for that genealogy website again. Get to work locating what you need, then drop off again for a few months.

129. **Don't Be Shy – Ask for a Discount!** Have you ever tried to cancel your television cable service and the company offers a huge discount, so you won't go to a competitor? Use the same technique when dealing with genealogy vendors. Don't accept the listed price on the website or in an email you receive when it is time to renew a subscription. Actually, <u>call</u> the company and get right to the point: ask if there is a discount for being a loyal customer. You might be surprised at the low price offered since the company wants to maintain its subscriber base; the cost to recruit new subscribers might allow for a discount to existing customers.

130. Leverage Coupon Websites. The genealogy business is not as insulated and small as you think! Many vendors such as Ancestry.com and others offer discounts and promo codes on the big coupon sites such as **Retail Me Not** (https://www.retailmenot.com/) and **Coupon Cabin** (https://www.couponcabin.com/). Always get in the habit of searching these sites BEFORE you use the Checkout option and plunk down your money!

131. Use Virtual Credit Card Numbers. Have you ever had a subscription service renew automatically especially when you decided you wanted to cancel? Most genealogy research sites force you to accept the auto-renew option (it is in the Terms of Service that, of course, you read before making your purchase, right?). One way around this is to go to your credit card or bank website and ask for a virtual credit card. By doing so, you can pay for a service from your bank or credit card, but the payment credentials won't allow more than one payment generation.

132. Access Your Local Library. A card at a public library can be your ticket to savings when it comes to genealogy research! More and more municipalities are providing access to Ancestry.com, fold3 and ProQuest as well as other subscriptions to their citizens. And don't think you have to use these databases in person at the library! Very often, after getting your library card, you can access sites from home.

133. **Stay Alert and Be Alerted!** Sign up for a vendor's newsletter where often you'll be the first to know about a new product or a discount. Also, if the site has a blog, make sure you subscribe to the posts either via email or RSS feed. Concerned about receiving too much junk email? Create a special email account at Google or Yahoo that you use just for signing up for deals and specials. Also learn how to use **Google Alerts** (https://www.google.com/alerts) to get notified: create alerts using keywords such as **genealogy** and **sale** or a **product name** and **sale**.

134. **Abandon Your Online Shopping Cart**. One trick to use is this: add items to a vendor's online shopping cart and let it sit for a few days. Then go in and "cancel" your cart. It is likely that the site will send you an email with a special discount to lure you back so you can finalize your purchase.

135. **Convert Gift Cards to Amazon Credit.** Are you sitting on several Visa or MasterCard gift cards with small balances? You can purchase an **Amazon E-Gift Card** (https://genealogybargains.com/amazon-giftcard) for an exact amount, like $7.54 and then use it to purchase genealogy books or other items on Amazon? A great way to make sure you don't lose money on those pre-paid debit/gift cards!

136. **Don't Be Afraid to Cancel.** Once you cancel a service, don't be surprised if they contact you and ask *why* you left. Be honest with them and tell them why. They may offer you a greatly discounted price or a free month of their service.

137. **Become An Affiliate.** If you run a website or a blog, you can sign up with many vendors to be an *affiliate* of that site. What does this mean? It means that you can earn money based on sales made through special links on your site. Many of the major genealogy vendors have these affiliate programs. **Amazon** has a program as well. You may not get rich, but you could earn enough money to offset costs.

138. **Avoid Impulse Decisions.** Just like shopping at the grocery store on an empty stomach, you need to use some common sense when making genealogy related purchases. When considering a purchase, even a small one (because the small ones add up, right?), set it aside and come back to the website or shopping cart a few hours or days later. Also, disable any "one click" shopping mechanisms like those used on **Amazon**. If the purchase process takes several steps, you are more likely to reconsider the purchase. It might turn out that the "must have" item is one quickly forgotten about in a few days.

139. **Get the Conference Discount.** Many genealogists attend national or state conferences which involve travel, hotel accommodations and other items - all costing money. Try to attend conferences that have a roommate matching service so you can split hotel costs if you are comfortable sharing a room. And what about volunteering? Many conferences are willing to either comp your registration or give you monetary credit towards the cost if you commit to a certain number of volunteer hours.

140. **Get the Senior Discount.** Again, it comes down to not being shy about asking. Here in the US, the American Association of Retired Persons or AARP, allows membership starting at age 50. And with membership comes huge discounts on many items, including an Ancestry.com subscription! **Ancestry AARP Discount** (https://www.genealogybargains.com/ancestry-aarp2).

141. **Check for Society Discounts.** Many genealogy societies and even professional organizations, including the **Association of Professional Genealogists** (https://www.apgen.org/ , offer discounts to their members.

142. **Check with Your Employer.** Did you know that The **Microsoft Workplace Discount Program** (https://www.microsoft.com/en-us/workplace-discount-program) lets you download Microsoft Office and other programs for a low one time price of as little as $9.95 USD? Your employer must use Microsoft products and services and also be enrolled in the program.

143. **Don't share login credentials**. Many services don't allow multiple logins using their credentials to access the site. Doing so is usually a violation of the Terms of Service for the site and you could find your account cancelled and you won't get a refund on what you paid. Websites can track your IP address and actually see if there is more than one login at a time. Don't take the chance of being banned from a genealogy website!

144. **Read the Terms of Service before you buy**. Fully understand how the website services work, especially if there is an auto-renew process. It is your responsibility to read all the text and to decide whether or not to use the site. If something isn't clear, email or call to get clarification.

145. Watch for Expiring Credits! Some sites allow you to purchase credits and use them as needed to download records. However, most credits expire after a set date, usually a year from purchase. Don't be caught short when it comes time to get that needed record and you're wondering what happened to all those credits!

146. Don't Try Multiple Intro Accounts. Many of the vendors have gotten smart to those who use different email addresses to sign up for a 7 or 14-day intro to a genealogy website. Most sites will track your IP address instead. Also, you'll likely receive a phone call from the service asking if you have any questions or need help with the site.

Getting Organized & Information Overload

Do you feel more overwhelmed than ever when it comes to genealogy and all the data you have access to these days? Remember back 10, 20 or 30 years ago – did it also feel like this or was data just more manageable back then?

Well, the feeling IS new and the reason? BIG DATA and the technologies that make more genealogy data available to us. With advances in technology, genealogy (and even non-genealogy) vendors now have the ability to produce more data and make it available to researchers.

The problem of keeping up with data is not going away nor will it be easily solved. Part of the burden is on the providers to make access to data easier and quicker. The other part is on us as researchers: we need to work smarter with the data!

147. Use a Project Management Template. Download my **Free Project Management Template** (https://genealogybargains.com/template-projmgmnt) and use an Excel spreadsheet to manage all your genealogy projects.

148. Join The Organized Genealogist group on Facebook. The Organized Genealogist (https://www.facebook.com/groups/organizedgenealogist/) is a Facebook group with over 43,000 members sharing tips and advice on organizing genealogy papers, files and more.

149. Prioritize items. A numbering system such as 1 = High Priority, 2= Medium Priority, and 3 = Low Priority can help you determine which items to tackle first.

150. Color code items. Consider using colors to indicate whether an item is overdue (red), on schedule (yellow) or completed (green).

151. Save online content NOW not LATER. Subscribe to the "I may not come this way again" school of thinking and never delay saving an image or file from an online site. Save it now, even if you have to dump it into a general folder for cataloging later. Websites and databases come and go!

152. Create files names that make sense. A file name should tell you the most important info about a file. "John Austin obit.pdf" is not as helpful as say "19770420 John Ralph Austin obit.pdf" which indicates the date of the obituary (April 20, 1977).

153. Do not overuse folders; rely on search. Do not waste too much time creating folders, sub-folders, and sub-sub-folders. Today's computers excel at indexing file data and allowing you to search for what you need. Think "Google" but only on your computer, not the Web.

154. Message Groups and Mailing Lists. Check out the **Ancestry Message Boards** (https://www.ancestry.com/boards/).

155. Use RSS feed readers. Ever wonder how some genealogists keep up with all the different blog posts and updates to websites? Smart family historians use a RSS feed reader such as **Feedly** (https://feedly.com/) and **Feeder** (https://feeder.co/reader) to stay on top of the latest news.

Giving Back

One of the hallmarks of the genealogy community is the generosity of its members when it comes to sharing resources and participating in collaborative problem solving. Here are some ways in which you can share your knowledge and expertise:

156. **Unclaimed Persons**. The group **Unclaimed Persons** (https://unclaimed-persons.org/) employs volunteer genealogists to help locate next of kin for unclaimed bodies sitting at county morgues.

157. **RAOGK**. Sign up as a volunteer at **Random Acts of Genealogical Kindness** (https://raogk.org/).

158. **Community Indexing**. Take a few hours each month to help index a set of records and make them available for research by all genealogists. Visit the **FamilySearch Indexing** site (https://www.familysearch.org/getinvolved/) and sign up today.

159. **Transcribing**. When visiting a repository or archive and locating documents related to your research, do this good deed once you get home: transcribe the documents and then send a copy of the transcription back to the repository as a "thank you."

160. **Offer your translating skills**. Are you fluent in another language? Do you have mad skillz when it comes to reading old Latin handwriting? Join **Genealogical Translations** (https://www.facebook.com/groups/GenealogicalTranslations/) group on Facebook and offer help when requested.

161. **Join various genealogy-related Facebook Groups**. Check out the **Genealogy on Facebook List** (https://socialmediagenealogy.com/genealogy-on-facebook-list/) maintained by Katherine Willson. You will find a group or page to cover every possible genealogy topic. Participate in conversations and assist other family historians.

Google

For many genealogists, Google is a search engine where you type what you're looking for and *voila!* links appear to other websites. But did you know that there are many more components in the Google family of applications and websites that can be used to amplify your research? Let's take a closer look at not only these often-neglected parts of Google, but we'll also discuss improving your search strategies when using the Google search engine.

Google Alerts

What if you could be notified when something new related to your genealogy was added to the Google index? Let's say someone started a new blog about an ancestral land, or added a website about a specific surname? Wouldn't it be nice if Google worked for you and sent you an email when new items appeared? That in essence is what Google Alerts can do: it is a notification service for any keyword search in Google.

162. **Setup Google Alerts to automate your web searches**. Create a **Google Account** then go to **Google Alerts** (https://www.google.com/alerts) and enter your search parameters.

163. **Test frequency of alerts**. Do not select "As it happens" under How often unless you are prepared to be bombarded with alerts via email. Try "Once a day" or "Once a week" to start.

164. **Set up foreign language alerts too!** To be alerted in another language make sure you are using the translated term for that language. Example: use **genealogie** instead of **genealogy** for German sites.

165. **Create "related website" alerts**. You can set up an alert for websites that are related to your website or a specific website. Use **related:websitename.com** as in **related: geneabloggers.com**.

166. **Track links to your blog or website**. Want to know when someone links to your blog or website? Use **link:websitename.com** as in **link:geneabloggers.com**.

167. **Specify locations**. Specify a location using state codes. Example **"land records" location:ok**.

168. **Use the RSS Feed option**. You can also select RSS Feed if you prefer to receive your alerts in an RSS Feed reader such as **Feedly**.

Google Books

See the **Books** section above for tips on Google Books.

Google Drive

Google Drive (formerly known as Google Docs) is a web-based application that allows you to create certain document types including spreadsheets, letters, presentations and more. Similar to Microsoft Office or other "suite" applications, Google Drive is free to use and access and allows you to share documents with other users.

169. **Accessing Google Drive**. You must have a Google account to use Google Drive. Go to https://drive.google.com/ and create a Google account.

170. **Creating a Google Drive Document**. In the **Sidebar** click **New** menu, click, and display the document types. Select **Document**. A blank document appears.

171. **Uploading Files to Google Drive**. In the **Sidebar** click **New** menu, click File Upload. Select file and click **Open**.

172. **Sharing Google Drive Documents**. Right-click over a document in Google Drive and select **Share**. Enter email address and select **Can Edit** or **Can View**.

Google Forms

173. **Create surveys using Google Forms**. Visit **Google Forms** (https://www.google.com/forms/about/) to create surveys for your genealogy society.

174. **Use Google Forms for indexing projects**. When indexing a record set, create a "user interface" for data input using Google Forms; all data is dumped into a common spreadsheet.

Google Images

175. **Use reverse image search to find similar images**. Go to **Google Images** (https://www.google.com/imghp) and click the camera icon for **Search by image**. Click **Upload an image** and upload your photo.

Google Newspapers

176. **Access over 25,000 free newspapers for free**. Visit **Google Newspapers** (https://news.google.com/newspapers)

177. **Use PrtScn to Save Google Newspaper Images.** Google has not made it easy to save articles found in Google Newspapers. Enlarge the page, hit the **PrtScn** button on your keyboard and then "paste" the image into a photo editor program. Also, consider using the **Microsoft Snipping Tool** (https://genealogybargains.com/microsoft-snippingtool) available in Windows.

Google Search Tricks

178. **Search for items within a specific site.** Enter the search criteria and then place "site:" in front of a domain name. Ex: **death records site:ancestry.com**.

179. **Search for similar sites.** To find sites similar to a specific site, use "related:" as in **related:ellisisland.org**.

180. **Use Google's Cache for "dead sites."** If you encounter the dreaded "404" error – Page Not Found – try to access a snapshot of the page taken by Google. Use "cache:" before the site name. Ex: **cache:ancestry.com**.

Google Translate

181. **Create a List of Genealogy Search Terms. Google Translate** (https://translate.google.com/) will translate English into over 133 languages and vice versa. Create a list of common genealogy terms (baptism, death certificate, marriage, etc.) in the language of your ancestors and then use them as search terms on Google or other search engines.

Mapping Your Genealogy

It is likely that as a genealogist you not only have a love of history and historical records, but also maps. So, what is it about this two-dimensional depiction of geography that fascinates us? Perhaps because very map could be a treasure map to help you unlock information about your family history and your ancestors.

Types of Maps

182. Census. These maps can help determine the proper enumeration district for an ancestor when indexed searching can't locate the census record. Also, ward maps were created during specific years and can help pinpoint where an ancestor was at a specific time.

183. **Data**. A relatively new type of map, almost always digital (online) which takes a data set, such as the expansion of slavery in the United States and depicts the data visually plotted against a geographical location. More and more of these "mashups" using "big data" are coming online each day.

184. **Fire Insurance**. Used to note buildings and their structure/composition, these maps also offer detailed descriptions of businesses, houses of worship and more – all helping us to better understand an ancestor's community.

185. **Historical**. A map showing how an area looked at a specific date or date range. Usually mark events such as statehood or war.

186. **Land**. Used to mark land ownership and how land parcels were determined and disbursed (on a state or federal basis).

187. **Political**. The most common map used by genealogists showing municipalities, names, streets, etc. Check the date of each map and use a date range to note changes.

188. **Topographical**. Also known as relief maps, show how the land looks via terrain, landmarks, features such as mountains, passes, meadows and more. These maps can often explain why your ancestor's family didn't attend church the closest church due to difficult terrain, etc.

189. **Transportation**. Determine travel routes, track growth of urban areas and understand migration patterns using transportation maps.

Genealogical Uses for Maps

From simply consulting a map to visualize an ancestor's location to actually plotting research data by location, you'll find that including maps in your research can actually solve research problems and help you break down brick walls.

190. **Check county and other borders.** When attempting to locate census and vital records, check to make sure you have the right locality especially county. County borders changed over time which impacts access to records.

191. **Review a variety of maps over time.** Compare various maps of the same area over the timespan of an ancestor's life – this is useful if maps designate landmarks, businesses, and roads. What was added or removed during that time period? Were locations "renamed" or changed?

192. **Plot location data for an ancestor.** Track where your ancestor lived, worshipped, worked, and more using maps. You will gain a better understanding as to the "why" of certain things such as "Why did she attend that church?"

193. **Use maps for cluster research.** Cluster research looks for groupings of people with the same surname, or those who are from a specific country or have a common ethnicity. Once identified, research those people for clues related to your own ancestor.

194. **Trace migration patterns.** Americans loved to move (and still do). Track migration of a family from one point to another. View the map to see what they encountered on their journey, what hardships they had to overcome and why they settled there.

Online and Offline Historic Map Resources

195. **American Civil War Maps**
https://americancivilwar.com/civil_war_map/

196. **Atlas of Historical County Boundaries**
https://digital.newberry.org/ahcb/

197. **Bureau of Land Management – GLO Records**
https://glorecords.blm.gov/

198. **Cyndi's List: Maps, Gazetteers & Geographical Information**
https://www.cyndislist.com/maps

199. **David Rumsey Map Collection**
https://www.davidrumsey.com/

200. **Digital Sanborn Maps**
https://digitalsanbornmaps.proquest.com/

201. **Google Maps**
https://www.google.com/maps

202. **Historic Map Works**
https://www.historicmapworks.com/

203. **Library of Congress: Maps**
https://www.loc.gov/maps/

204. **Mapping History**
https://mappinghistory.uoregon.edu/

205. **Perry-Castañeda Library Map Collection**
https://maps.lib.utexas.edu/maps/

206. **Pinmaps**
https://www.pinmaps.net/

207. **United States Digital Map Archive - USGenWeb**
http://usgwarchives.net/maps/

Photos

208. Photo Resources for Genealogists. Access this resource board at Pinterest (https://www.pinterest.com/genealogybargains/photo-resources-for-genealogists/) for free photo editors, watermarking apps, and more.

Metadata

Metadata is "data about data" and is a way of classifying and organizing files including digital images. A better definition of metadata might be "constructed information," meaning a classification of various data points about a file. It is available on many different types of files including photo files such as JPG, TIFF, and PNG.

The main advantage of metadata is its portability, meaning that when the file is emailed to another person or posted online, the metadata stays with the file. Sort of like having a virtual sticky note that travels with a photo and tells you more about who is in the photo, where it was taken, etc.

209. **Add tags to photos, documents, and files**. Tagging or labeling is a way of organizing and categorizing files. Consider tags such as surnames, location names, time periods, record sets such as "Henneberg; 1920 Census; Bronx." Once added you can use the search function to locate similarly tagged items.

210. **Add a copyright statement to files**. One way to trace the use of your original work is to add a brief copyright statement in the Comments section of the file's metadata. Most users are not aware of metadata, and this can offer a way to trace the origination of a photo or document you locate on the Internet.

211. **Add a source citation to a file**. If a file represents a copy of a record, consider placing the source citation in the Comments section of the file's metadata. Then you can always determine how the document was located and when.

212. **Geotag a location.** Note where you took a photograph, maybe of a grave or ancestors' homes. There are many programs that can help you do this and then easily upload the photos to Google Earth placing them in the proper location.

Photo Gifts

213. **MyHeritage Reimagine**
https://genealogybargains.com/reimagine

214. **15 Creative Photo Display Ideas That Don't Need Frames**
https://www.artifactuprising.com/diy/display-photos-without-frames

215. 27 Unique Photo Display Ideas That Will Bring Your Memories To Life
https://www.buzzfeed.com/maitlandquitmeyer/unique-photo-display-ideas-that-will-bring-your-memories

216. DIY Family Tree Chalkboard
https://www.yourhomebasedmom.com/diy-family-tree-chalkboard-2/

217. Family History: Crafts
https://www.pinterest.com/valerieelkins/family-history-crafts/

218. Family Photo Blocks
https://divaofdiy.com/easy-handmade-photo-gift/

219. Picture Frame Memory Wreath
https://www.infarrantlycreative.net/picture-frame-memory-wreath/

Scanning Photos

The best way to preserve photos is to first make sure you have a scanned digital copy that is high resolution.

220. Clean the glass on the scanner before each use.

221. Carefully position the photo and align it with the scanner guides before scanning. This is easier than having to "rotate" the image using photo editing software after the scan.

222. Do not remove photos that are glued into scrapbooks or from those "magnetic" photo albums. Scan the entire page and then crop the photos you want.

223. Always scan at the highest possible resolution, 300 dpi ("dots per inch") minimum, 600 dpi preferred.

224. After scanning, create a copy of each digital image file, add the word "MASTER" to the file name, and place these in a separate folder. Then work with the other file to make edits, color correction, cropping. This way you always have a master copy for use in case you make a mistake during the editing process.

225. Place a dark piece of cloth, such as velvet, on top of the photo to block out ambient light.

226. Once the image is scanned, look to preserve the item using sound archival materials that will not lead to further deterioration.

Pinning Your Family History

It seems that pinning sites are all the rage and becoming more popular. Sites like Pinterest and others can let you share your family history with family, friends, and the public. But be warned! Pinning can become an addictive way to surf the Web!

Besides Pinterest, sites like Google My Maps, Google Collections, What Was There, History Pin and uencounter.me allow you to share your family photos and content easily! And you never know who will find that content and how you might connect with other genealogists. Pinning is the new "cousin bait!"

227. Content = your uploaded content OR found, curated content. We have heard that "content is king" but what do we mean by family history content that can be "pinned?" There are two types: your own scanned content in the form of photos, documents, ephemera, etc. OR content that you "find" on the Internet from blogs, websites and even within the pinning platform itself.

228. Copyright and Pinning. The best approach is to always pin your own original content (and include a copyright notice in the text). Or "repin" content already available on Pinterest. For other sites, see if they have posted a Pinterest button or a means to share the content on social media sites. If so, and they encourage sharing, use those devices to share content with others. The big "no-no" is downloading an image then uploading or pinning it as your own. Doing so is a sure fire way to get in trouble.

229. Get Permission Before Using Family Pictures and Other Items. Pinning information about living people should be done with caution, especially if it discloses private information. Ask family members and tell them how you intend to use the image and the information.

230. Use Social Media. Share your pins with family and others via Facebook, Twitter, and other social media platforms. Also make sure you understand what happens when you automate the process! Many of these apps will access more than just your pinned content and will be able to pin or post on your behalf.

What to Pin?

231. Family Stories: Did you first get interested in genealogy based on stories you heard told at family events and reunions? Such stories can be brief and include a photo. Other family members can add their comments.

232. Recipes and Stories About Food. Fond family memories are often generated when a secret family recipe or favorite dish is highlighted. Pin images from old cookbooks, and family celebrations.

233. Family Timelines. Similar to creating a storyboard, pin images important to a person's life then describe the events.

234. Memorialize Ancestors and Places. Create a memorial with pins about a person's life or to places from a time gone by.

235. Share Resources. Build a toolbox of resources for any topic including genealogy and family history. Pin blog posts and websites that would help other researchers.

Pinning Sites You Should Know

236. Pinterest. The most popular pinning site, **Pinterest** (https://www.pinterest.com/) allows you to build online boards – similar to bulletin boards – on which you post or "pin" items of interest.

237. Google Maps. Many people use **Google Maps** (https://maps.google.com) for driving directions or to view the location of a business, but one feature that is important to genealogists is customized personal maps containing pinned information.

238. **What Was There.** Pinning to **What Was There** (https://www.whatwasthere.com) is based on a street address, and then uploading images and pinning them to a map driven by Google Maps.

239. **History Pin**. Based in the UK, **History Pin** (https://www.historypin.com) works just like *What Was There* and is also based on Google Maps.

Playing Nice in the Genealogy Sandbox

You think it would be simple especially since the genealogy community is generally known as a dedicated and intelligent group of researchers all focused on a similar goal: finding our ancestors. Yet researchers are people and as such little things like the ego and even misinformation or lack of knowledge can be like sand in the gears of the genealogy machine.

Getting What You Need From Family Members

Family members are an important part of the genealogy research process especially since they are often our starting point on the genealogy journey. As you mature as a genealogist and become better at research, you may find the need to not just get more information, but more precise information from relatives.

240. **Use the best contact method**. Understand that some family members do not respond well to technology so a phone call or in-person interview might be best. For others, especially those that are busy, email is best.

241. **Do not frame the discussion**. Very often, if we get too specific in terms of what we need we miss other information the person is sitting on (example: "I need the death location for Aunt Hildegard"). Prompts are good for an interview but keep them general and open-ended.

242. **Communicate clearly and concisely**. "Get in and get out," is one way to look at it. You can do this efficiently and effectively, yet still be personable.

243. **Bring technology to your interview**. Many relatives do not want to part with photos, documents and other items that are relevant to their family history. With today's technology including mobile scanners and mobile apps, you should be able to record interviews and digitize documents while you are working with your family members.

244. **Honor and respect**. No matter if they are your elders, younger or a very distant relative whom you have never met . . . they deserve respect. Make sure you ask if they have time to talk on the phone. Remember that they may be talking about a difficult time in their own lives or those of their parents or siblings.

245. **Say "thank you."** Especially if you have conducted a long interview or if the relative has provided you with a large amount of information, send a thank you note (handwritten, of course) and perhaps copies of some old photographs or a printed version of your research.

How to Deal with Librarians, Archivists, and Others

Have you had difficult encounters with the folks I call "The Gatekeepers" of records? These are the librarians, the court clerks, the archivists, and others. I believe there are many more good interactions than bad ones, but guess which ones we remember?

246. **Employees or volunteers, they are still people.** Whether you are dealing with a government civil servant, a staff member of a library or even a volunteer, remember that they are just like you. Good days, bad days, etc. You should not tolerate rudeness but try to keep everything in perspective.

247. **Find common ground.** Likely, the archivist or librarian is a researcher just like you. In addition, just like you, they are asked to assist others with their research goals. Respect their education, their intelligence, and their role in the organization. And they will respect you as well. "If people deal with the general public, they've probably seen it all. If they eventually know you, you're not the public."

248. **Call ahead.** Make sure you know the exact location and hours of operation for the specific day you will be at the repository. Also, ask for the name of the best person to talk to once you arrive. Briefly tell them what you are looking for (avoid "The Story") and they might surprise you by having resources ready and waiting.

249. **Understand the rules and the setup.** This means reading the regulations on the website, but also asking for a printed copy when you arrive; keep in mind that they may have changed. Get to know the layout of the repository and watch what other researchers do, especially the "regulars" (see below).

250. **Remember the 5 Cs: Clear, Concise, Complete, Congenial, and Compensation.** Avoid telling "The Story" when requesting records. You know what I mean: the story of your ancestor, where they lived, who they married, etc. Curt Witcher, Senior Manager for Special Collections at the Allen County Public Library in Ft. Wayne, Indiana, advocates following the 5 Cs to get what you need as a researcher. "Your question or inquiry should be no longer than you can hold a lit match before you must blow it out." Another genealogist offers: "We need to have librarians, archivists, record custodians, and information managers working for us. Know when to tell how much! State your request up front. Do not start with a long story. They do not care about your family. Have a research plan before arriving. Then articulate it. Brevity and clarity are golden. Talk in a courthouse like a lawyer, not a genealogist. In other words, say 'I am looking for a deed.' No need to tell your entire story."

251. **Why a donation matters**. One of my favorite genealogists once said that whenever she researches at a church or synagogue or other religious institution, she always has a small donation ready in an envelope. Even if you are not a member of that institution, realize that their staff are taking time out of their duties to help. When asking for records in writing, send a check with your request and let them know that you appreciate their assistance. Also, not all donations are monetary: have you considered transcribing a document you are using and then sending them the transcription?

252. Who's the boss? One approach is to recognize the skill of the gatekeeper and respect their knowledge and position. If you get "stuck" and cannot get what you want because the person is not properly trained or is not aware of the access regulations, talk with the supervisor. However, do not do it to embarrass the one who is short on knowledge . . . instead, focus on improving the process for you, the repository and for other researchers.

253. Befriend a "regular." This means after a few visits note the other researchers that are always there. Establish a relationship and let them show you the ropes. Soon you will be a "regular" too.

254. The gift conundrum. The classic "bring cupcakes" ploy is not as straightforward a solution as it seems. Be careful with any gift giving. In some places, employees cannot accept gifts of any kind or gifts over a certain value. Instead consider a donation especially if it is a non-profit organization. Also, get to know the gatekeepers at a repository first. Then you may want to bring a gift as a thank you or even ask one of them out for coffee or lunch, so they get to know you and your research goals.

255. Know your rights. As a genealogist, a researcher, and a member of the public, you should have the same access rights to records as the next person, especially in a government office that has open records regulations. Again, do your homework, print out the regulations, but do not go in ready to rumble. If you encounter a situation where you are barred from access, take notes including the date, time, and the person to whom you spoke and what was said. Ask to see a supervisor. If the person _is_ the supervisor, then disengage and when you get home call, email, or write to someone at the agency who can resolve the complaint.

Correcting Information in a Collaborative Environment

256. Understand the capabilities of the platform. When dealing with websites that display family trees or indexed/transcribed records, do your homework and determine what can and what can't be done. This may include having to read the Terms of Service agreement to understand who owns user data once it is uploaded.

257. Ask and ask nicely. When dealing with other researchers online, a "virtual" smile goes a long way. Let the other person know that you have found other information related to a specific person, place or event and ask them if they would like the data for their own research. Also, ask them to update any online postings not to prove that your research is "correct" but to help genealogists who come upon the research in the future.

258. Avoid "right" and "wrong" statements. The easiest way to alienate a fellow genealogist is to tell them that their research is wrong. Even if the research is incorrect, your goal should be to improve the current research and to help future researchers.

259. If necessary, publish your own research. Sometimes either you cannot contact the other genealogist, or they refuse to update their information. Remember that you have at your disposal a variety of tools to make sure your research is just as visible as any other genealogist.

Giving and Receiving Proper Credit

First, realize that facts cannot be copyrighted (meaning birth dates, death dates, names, etc.) But narrative text, say in a genealogy report that you put together, is protected by copyright. Even so, if you get a great lead on your own research from what someone else has posted, here is some advice:

260. **Contact the researcher, if possible.** State how you want to use the research (especially if you intend to publish the information in print or online in a blog or website), show how you will credit the researcher and then thank them for their hard work.

261. **Build a relationship.** Briefly mention how you are related to the research, or if representing a client, how your client is related.

262. **Stick to the facts and cite your sources.** Again, if it is facts, then technically you can use the information. However, if it were sourced, I would do the research myself and then use the facts as I wanted. Make sure your source citations states when you find the record!

263. **Write your own narrative.** If the person refuses to give permission to use their narrative, realize that they have that right. You will need to do your own narrative; sorry, there is no shortcut here!

264. **Reference, but do not plagiarize.** For research, you can reference that person's research with a footnote as long as you do not reproduce the entire text.

265. **Advocate and educate.** Often, these situations occur with new genealogists who do not understand copyright or the need to give credit. Be courteous and let them know that you need attribution and why.

266. **Be steadfast.** Occasionally you will find a person who knew what they were doing and did not care. Hold your ground. Research your options and remember to pick your battles. Is a confrontation – either online or in person – really worth it?

The Do's and Don'ts of Collaborating and Sharing

267. Be nice. The world is a small town. The genealogy community is really a small place, and you realize that more and more with the advent of social media. Rude genealogists are duly noted, and their reputation will precede them. Kindness offered to others is often returned ten-fold.

268. Ask for attribution and give attribution. If you want your work to be credited, make sure you are walking the walk on attribution. Drafting the text, sending it to the researcher, and getting their approval is a nice gesture. Also, do not be afraid to set some reasonable rules when providing your research and always ask for attribution. Again, providing the ready-made text that credits your work not only makes it easier, but can also help educate the other researcher if they are a newbie.

269. Do not give to get. It can be difficult to embrace an abundance model, but once you start to share with others, you get the hang of how it works. Do not fall into the "tit for tat" game, but do not be a sucker either.

270. Track your work. Use Google Alerts to track your copyrighted content. Some tricks: create a unique phrase for each document or intentionally misspell a word in a phrase and use these as your search string.

Genealogy Conflict Resolution

271. Step back and research! That's right – research! In addition, I do not mean to take a break and do some genealogy research. I mean research the chain of events and the facts the brought you and the other person to the conflict. Genealogists are smart cookies and there is no reason we cannot apply our analytical skills to these situations as well.

272. **Make a peace offering; offer a cease-fire.** Sounds like we are at war, right? Sometimes you just need to lay it out in person, in writing or in an email such as: "We disagree about _____ and I respect your opinion. I feel there are many more benefits to working together than against one another. I'd like to resolve our conflict as follows . . ." Doing so does not mean you are operating from a point of weakness. It means you are a smart operator.

273. **Some bridges will just be burned.** In some cases, no matter how nice you are to another person, you cannot salvage the relationship. Walk away and disengage. Remember that you can still disagree and yet still be "right" and true to your principles and standards.

274. **Capitalize on energy.** A little secret about story writing that actually is pertinent to this topic as well as genealogy: conflict brings about change and things happen. There is energy in conflict. You just need to learn how to channel it effectively. Do not get wrapped up in drama that can wear you out.

275. **Be professional.** This means be courteous if you run into the person at a genealogy event or you both serve on a society committee or board. Do not get baited into an argument. Always seek the high road.

276. **Seek arbitration.** You may belong to a genealogy organization that offers a conflict resolution service. Take advantage of it.

277. **Guard your reputation.** Just because you are not in "right relationship" with another genealogist, doesn't mean they have the right to damage your reputation. Setting up a Google Alert for your name is not paranoia; it is smart use of technology.

Potpourri – What They Never Tell You about Genealogy

Black Sheep and the Dark Side of Genealogy

278. **Do not get too comfortable**. Remember that you may stumble upon some shocking and disturbing information when researching your roots. Understand the best ways to preserve what you find and share (or not share) it with family members. A good start is to read ***Family History Begins at the End of Your Comfort Zone*** (https://familyhistorydaily.com/tips-and-tricks/family-history-begins-at-the-end-of-your-comfort-zone/)

Collateral and Cluster Searching

279. **Always use a research log**. Make sure you enter your finds in a research log, no matter how insignificant they may seem at the time. Remember, you are looking for data that will indirectly provide clues to your direct lines.

280. **Formulate theories . . . and write them down!** How often have you contemplated certain theories about your research, only to forget them later? Make sure there is a "Possible theories" or "Notes" section in your research log. You will find it easier to recall those ideas later on if you enter them right away.

281. **Spelling counts! Nevertheless, not in the way you expect it to . . .** Make sure you are employing spelling variations when conducting each search. Surnames changed over time.

282. **Stop relying on records that are indexed**. The indexing process is not perfect and if you rely solely on your ability to find information through a search, you cannot conduct an effective collateral or cluster search.

283. **Search by address**. You might be surprised at who lived at a particular address before or after your ancestor was there.

284. **Leave no stone unturned**. Be dedicated in your search efforts to perform a "reasonably exhaustive search." If you don't, you are only shortchanging yourself.

285. **Search without boundaries**. Make sure you are searching over that county or state line if an ancestor lived in an area close to a border.

Finding the Living

286. **Use "people search" engines**. In the United States, many records related to living persons are accessible and open to the public. While most require a trip to a governmental office, many can be found online for free or a small fee. Check out **ZabaSearch** (https://www.zabasearch.com/), one of the most popular people finder sites.

287. Making contact: Expect hesitancy. While contacting living people via telephone is preferred, understand that the person who answers might feel you are a scammer. Consider sending an email with links to your blog or website in order to build legitimacy. Alternatively, send a letter, providing the recipient with your contact information. Let them contact you if and when they feel comfortable.

Name Variations

288. Have You Guessed the Name? Don't laugh . . . check out *Guessing a Name Variation* (https://www.familysearch.org/en/wiki/Guessing_a_Name_Variation) at FamilySearch for proven steps that can work!

289. Nicknames – What Do They Mean? Check out the *List of Traditional Nicknames in Historic Documents* (https://www.familysearch.org/en/wiki/Traditional_Nicknames_in_Old_Documents_-_A_Wiki_List#List_of_Traditional_Nicknames_in_Historic_Documents) at FamilySearch.

290. Try swapping given and middle names. For many different reasons, individuals may have used different names at different times in their life. Search based on both given and middle names and search using different orders.

291. Spelling Counts . . . Sort Of! Try your searches using different spellings for names. See *Spelling Substitution Tables for the United States & Canada* (https://www.familysearch.org/en/wiki/Spelling_Substitution_Tables_for_the_United_States_and_Canada) at the FamilySearch Research Wiki.

Preserving Family History

Many of us got our start in tracing and preserving our family history based on a story, perhaps one you heard as a child. Do you remember how engaging that story was? Was it the story itself or how the storyteller presented the information? Whatever the reasons, the story had an impact and if not preserved on paper or in an audio recording, that story is somehow preserved in your mind.

Fast forward to the 21st century and it seems that "what's old is new again" with storytelling one of the hot buzzwords. The fact is that oral history and storytelling as it involves family and ancestry has been around ever since humans walked the earth. Before writing forms existed and even as recently as the early 20th century with a lack of vital records, family history was preserved as oral history.

Communication and Scheduling

292. **Determine who you want to interview**, list the reasons why, and schedule possible dates and locations.

293. **Also, determine the best way to contact the interview subject.** Older relatives who do not know you personally will not respond well to a phone call. Consider using another relative such as a cousin who knows them better to "broker" a connection and help set up the interview.

294. **Schedule the date and time of the interview and the location.** Make sure the location is quiet and free from distractions. If it is a long distance interview over Skype, the broker suggestion above might be a good idea, especially if the person being interviewed is not familiar with this technology.

295. **Send your invitation** and outline the reason for the interview and the types of questions to ask.

296. **Make it clear to the interview subject as to how the interview will be conducted and what devices you will be using.** Also, elaborate on how you plan to structure the interview. For example, let your subject know that you plan to ask one question at a time and that you would like a five-minute or less response to each question.

297. **Manage your expectations.** Reassure the person being interviewed that you are not expecting perfectly thought-out phrasing. Emphasize that you are looking for a story and pattern of speech that best reflects them and their life history.

298. Check to see if you will have access to a wireless Internet connection during the interview. This is important if you are using any cloud service or other platforms to upload content.

Recording Devices and Platforms

299. Always review the instructions on how to use each device and platform. Also, practice using the device before the actual interview.

300. Bring batteries and a power supply or necessary charging devices!

301. Have a backup plan in case a device or platform does not work. Remember you may have worked hard to schedule the interview and you may only have once chance at this!

302. Make sure your interview subject is comfortable with the recording device or platform. If there is a possibility that the interview subject could be confused by the technology, consider buying an old-fashioned phone handset that plugs into the "high tech" device. Some of these inexpensive handsets come with noise reduction technologies that can overcome background noise.

Interview Questions and Prompts

303. Create a list of questions to use during the interview. Make sure you have a printed copy of the questions as well as an electronic version (PDF) on an iPad, tablet computer or other device.

304. For older interview subjects, print each question on an index card or piece of paper with large font. Also, include a relevant image that might prompt a response.

305. **Consider sending the questions in advance**. Some people prefer knowing the questions before the interview so that they can think about (but not rehearse) their responses.

306. **Do not forget to bring old family photographs** since these will often invoke memories.

307. **Create a master list of questions** and then sort the questions into grouped themes. You may not be able to cover all questions in one interview, so use one theme for one interview, another for the next, etc.

Sharing Methods and Platforms

308. **You do not need to have a sharing method or platform selected prior to the interview**; however, some interview subjects would like to know exactly what kind of "end product" you hope to produce.

309. **Make a list of different ways you hope to preserve and share your interview content**. Spend time with each one and focus on those that are easy to use and produce the best results.

Tips and Tricks for Interviewing Family Members

310. **Be prepared**. Make sure you have all your equipment and your questions or prompts. There are times when an opportunity for an interview pops up unexpectedly. Make sure you are adept at improvising; having an app like **Saving Memories Forever** on your smartphone is good insurance!

311. **Ask permission**. Keep track of your time and if necessary, ask if you can extend the interview. If using a digital recorder or smartphone app, ask permission of the interview subject and take time to explain the tool or the process.

312. **One question at a time**. Do not bunch several questions together into one long question. Short, open-ended questions asked one at a time work best.

313. **Fly solo (mostly)**. Plan to do the interview in a one-on-one format. Sometimes having others around can be inhibiting unless you are at a family gathering such as a wedding or a holiday meal. Especially when dealing with difficult topics, make sure that the interview subject is comfortable telling their story with those in the room.

314. **Use the grandkids.** Sometimes it can be difficult to get older family members to answer questions. Consider using the grandchildren to ask the questions. No grandparent can resist telling his or her story to an interested child.

315. **Multiple interview subjects help to focus on relationships**. Having two or more people as part of an interview can allow for a natural exchange of comments and those comments in turn give some insight into the relationship between those people.

316. **Use props**. Photos and family mementos are great to elicit stories and bring back memories. Bring the props out one by one.

317. **Do not interrupt**. If inspiration strikes and you think of a good question, jot it down and save it for another part of the interview.

318. **Do not challenge inaccurate information**. During a response to a question, you may see that the information offered conflicts with your research or what others have offered. Do not contradict and do not challenge. You will have time to process the information and to put it into context of your family's history later on as you compile and prepare the contents for preservation and sharing.

319. **Do not tire out your subject**. Most interviews should be one hour or less in length with a max of 90 minutes. Saving Memories Forever suggests that the response to each question should take about five minutes and that the entire interview should last no longer than 45 minutes. In reality, the interview should stop when you first see that your subject is getting tired. Remember, you want the interview to be a positive experience and possibly lead to future interviews.

320. **Redirect and bring them back**. Sometimes a person will go off on a tangent and speak about a topic that is not relevant. Deftly and gently, bring them back around to the original question. Having the question written down and in a position where the interviewee can refer to it will also help with focus.

321. **Check the time**. If you and your subject have agreed on a set end time, respect this and schedule another interview if necessary.

322. **Do not frame the discussion**. If your research shows that a person was hard to live with or perhaps had difficult relations with others, do not offer those details on the initial question. See what the interview subject responds with and follow-up with "Well, I heard . . ." or "Uncle Charles told me that . . ." and offer your evidence.

323. **Silence counts**. It is fine if your interview subject is silent for a short time; generating memories is hard work! These gaps can be edited out later on.

324. **Do not interrogate**. Some older relatives may not offer up names and dates in the beginning; do not pepper them with questions. Circle back with questions such as "What was Aunt Cora's maiden name?"

325. Do not show off. The interview is not about you and your skills. Your family member is the star so let their star shine.

Follow Up Materials

326. Send a thank you note or email or make a phone call to thank the interview subject for their time.

327. Review content. If you are publishing the interview in print or some other format, consider offering the interview subject a chance to review the content first.

328. Transcribe oral interviews when you have time. Consider using a program to do this or send it out to a transcribing service.

329. Send a copy of the final published work to the interview subject.

Organizing and Producing Your Family's Story

330. Take Inventory of Your Content. Whether your project is large or small, make sure you have a way to track what you have so you know what you need. Develop a labeling system, perhaps color-coded based on the type of element or a numbering system. Use a spreadsheet or a digital document online to track items.

331. Create a Project and Task List. Going from wanting to interview an older interview to actually having the interview complete and preserved can involve lots of work and many steps. Use a spreadsheet to outline each element and mark them off your list. Use the same approach for the overall project of preserving a family story.

332. Modularize the Story via Story Boarding. While index or flash cards may seem "old fashioned" the concept of breaking down a story into elements or segments works and is a proven tactic for telling stories. If you are working on a story about your grandfather's arrival in the United States, break the story down into elements such as background, life in the old country, preparing to leave, the trip, etc. You can arrange the elements in different orders if needed. In addition, do not forget that index cards have gone digital!

333. Use a Timeline. When focusing on one person or a specific time period, you may want to use a timeline program not just to place facts of the story in order, but more importantly to see other historical events running parallel to your family story. In addition, many of these timelines can be published to images and used in your preserved family history.

Cleaning or Consolidating a Home

334. Consider temporary storage. Very often, you will not have the leisure of taking your time sorting through items. Rather than toss items that you will regret later on, arrange for temporary storage that is secure and designed to protect items against water or other damage. Check for discounts and read the contract to make sure you understand what happens to the items if the rental charges are not paid.

335. Set up a system and set some ground rules. Those who have been through the clean-up process recommend going room by room as a group, rather than having everyone in their own room. Also clearly communicate how items will be documented and handled.

336. **Designate a "command center" or "control area."** If you are keeping an inventory, taking photos, assembling boxes, using markers for writing, etc., then designate an easily accessible area where everyone involved can find these items. Set up a card table in a room or use a kitchen counter. Also, make it clear that certain items should not leave the "control area" at any time.

337. **Take a quick inventory**. When you first get started, write down a quick inventory by room and note the major items. Keep the notebook handy to add items as you work.

338. **Use video**. Use a video camera or the video app on your smartphone to record what is in each room and closet before you start. Not every "clean-up" situation is pleasant and if family members bring up issues or questions, you can prove what was in the home before you started cleaning.

339. **"Touch It Once"** This is an approach used by many who clean out houses: the idea is to minimize moving items around the house. Pick up an item, decide and then act on it . . . once. This is not always possible, but it is a worthy goal.

340. **Look EVERYWHERE**! You have seen stories in the news of a desk bought at Goodwill that had $90,000 in cash stuff underneath, right? Keep in mind that an Alzheimer's patient will store items in the most bizarre places . . . my mother decided to use gold bracelets for bookmarks! Go through every wadded up napkin or tissue. Leaf through every book. Look underneath furniture including chairs and desks. Check baseboards, carpets, and old pipes. Other areas where items have been found include ice cube trays, flour and sugar canisters, taped underneath drawers . . . Once

you sell the home, legally the buyer can claim possession of any items found.

341. **Who wants copies of photos**? One way to track who wants a digital copy of a photo is to place a sticky note on the back with the names of those wanting a copy. Others have used a similar envelope system. Make sure you do not write on the sticky note while it is on the photo or on the envelope with the photo inside – you may damage the photo!

Converting Old Media

It is likely that you are sitting on a stockpile of home movies, slides, video tapes and even tape recordings related to family history. Alternatively, you may have access to these treasures through another family member. The challenge for most of us is how to access the memories hidden in these media forms, especially since we may not have the devices to view the information.

342. **Convert items yourself**. The DIY method can save you money and allows you to review content either as it is being converted or right afterwards. However, you may have to purchase a device (like a scanner for photo negatives) which you will only use once. In addition, you may need to learn new technical skills in order to ensure the best resolution and quality of the final converted product.

343. Use a service or vendor to convert items. Sending items out for conversion can save time and be more cost effective with a large number of items. In addition, the vendor, such as **Larsen Digital** (https://larsendigital.com/thomas/), is often an expert in the type of media and will deliver a higher quality converted product than you could produce at home. However, with thousands of slides or hundreds of home movies, the cost can be prohibitive, and you can only review the results once the converted media is delivered.

After You're Gone

In summary, here are some tips of future proofing your genealogy research and making sure it is preserved for others to use for generations to come:

344. Take inventory. Determine what you have, and this includes hard copy as well as digital assets and online sites.

345. Include in estate planning. Create a codicil to your will or make sure there are some form of instructions concerning your genealogy research.

346. Backup your data. Backing up your genealogy data is a good habit for the living, and it will keep all your info in one place for your executor.

347. Futureproof your technology. CD-ROM discs degrade over time. Negatives and movies can fade and fall apart. Transfer items to digital ASAP.

348. Have that conversation with family. Be very clear about where your genealogy research is located, why it is important, and what you want done with it.

349. Contact organizations. Determine which libraries, societies and archives will accept all or part of your collection. Donate items you don't need NOW.

350. Post items online. Consider starting a blog – even a private one – to preserve your family stories. Do the same with a family tree on Ancestry or one of the popular genealogy sites.

351. Do stuff NOW. Tell your own stories NOW. Write that genealogy book NOW. Interview family members NOW.

Research Logs and Methodology

352. **Read up on genealogy methodology.** Go beyond mere name collecting; understand how to collect and evaluate evidence properly. Recommended books: ***Advanced Genealogy Research Techniques*** (https://genealogybargains.com/amazon-advgenrestech), ***Genealogy Standards*** (https://genealogybargains.com/amazon-genstandards), and ***Mastering Genealogical Proof*** (https://genealogybargains.com/amazon-mastgenproof).

353. **Use a Research Log.** Download a **Genealogy Research Log** for Excel (https://genealogybargains.com/genreslog) and track your research before you enter it into any genealogy database software such as Family Tree Maker.

354. **Cite Your Sources**. Invest in *Evidence Explained: Citing History Sources from Artifacts to Cyberspace* (https://genealogybargains.com/amazon-evidenceexplained) or for smaller budgets, *QuickSheet: Your Stripped-Bare Guide to Citing Sources* (https://genealogybargains.com/amazon-citing-sources-quicksheet) Understand the basics of how to cite sources. Also, consider joining **Genealogy – Cite Your Sources** on Facebook (https://www.facebook.com/groups/Citesources/).

355. **Check out Bibliography Generators**. A variety of programs, many of them free, offer the ability to cite sources and generate a bibliography. These include **BibMe** (https://www.bibme.org/), **Citation Machine** (https://www.citationmachine.net/) **EasyBib** (https://www.easybib.com/), and **Zotero** (https://www.zotero.org/).

356. **Most genealogy software programs have source citation templates**. Before re-inventing the wheel, check your favorite genealogy program to see if they have source citation templates available for use.

357. **Evidence Evaluation Apps and Software**. Consider evaluating your genealogy research data using software such as **Clooz** (https://clooz.com/), **Evidentia** (https://evidentiasoftware.com/), and **ResearchTies** (https://researchties.com/).

Self-Publishing

358. Access Self-Publishing Toolbox. Check out the **Self-Publishing Toolbox** on Pinterest (https://www.pinterest.com/genealogybargains/self-publishing-toolbox/) or download it via PDF (https://genealogybargains.com/syllabus-selfpublish) .

359. The Self-Publishing Process. The process of publishing your own book or guide is similar to conventional publishing except that you agree to take on many of the tasks handled by the publisher. The process outline below assumes that your digital manuscript is finalized and proofread.

- Determine publishing format – print, e-book, or both
- Select self-publishing platform
- Prepare marketing materials including author bio, press release, book description
- Secure images for marketing and book cover design
- Design book cover – send out design request or do it yourself

- Review proof copy
- Publish – print and/or e-book version
- Market book
- Collect royalties and determine costs

360. **Understand the term "Print on Demand."** Print on demand means that you as an author or publisher are not warehousing or storing copies of your book to be mailed to purchasers. When you use a print on demand service like **Lulu** (https://lulu.com), you let the purchaser order the book and Lulu takes care of collecting payment, sending out the item and then sending you the money. Of course, these services do take a cut – up to 30% of the purchase price.

361. **Benefits of Self-Publishing.** There are many benefits to a DIY approach for your next publication:
    - Usually, the royalty rate for self-published works is much higher.
    - Offers more control over the process.
    - As publisher, you retain all rights to the work.
    - No long-term contracts with publishers.
    - Shorter turn-around time compared to conventional publishing.
    - Print on demand options avoid the need to warehouse books or have large runs.
    - Offers the ability to sell works online via Amazon and other booksellers.

362. **Self-Publishing Do's and Don'ts.** Here is a list of issues involved with self-publishing your work:
    - Don't be afraid to spend money on a service that will assist you in converting your conventionally published work to self-published and e-book format.
    - Use a platform that is easy to use and has the best marketing options.

- Go slow – don't try to produce large books, quickly and in many formats. The result will be sloppy and could affect your reputation.
- If also creating an e-book using e-reader formats, start with plain text or minimal formatting. Produce the e-book first, and then add formatting for PDF/printed version.
- Look for a platform that will provide an ISBN number for free or at a reasonable price. If your work is already conventionally published, you may be able to transport your ISBN number to the new format.
- Have your book proofed by another set of eyes or hire a copy editor.
- Once published, seek out influential community members and vendors to review your book.

Smarter Search Strategies for Genealogy

Many genealogists begin their research online and are often frustrated with the lack of results. The cause might not be a lack of records at the specific site, but the way you're performing the search! While basic search techniques work on most genealogy sites, you need to power up your search skills to get the most out of niche genealogy websites and uncover those hidden record sets!

363. Use search tips for each database. Ancestry has a set of search tips for each of its databases. Scroll to the bottom of the page and in the About section you will find a Search Tips link with helpful information. For the US World War I Draft Cards database at Ancestry, here is a tip: "Men who resided in British territories sometimes listed themselves simply as British citizens without noting their origin in Canada, Australia, Ireland, Jamaica, etc."

364. **Use wild card searching.** The asterisk (*) and question mark (?) are the most common wildcards for searching. Use * for a range of characters and use ? for a specific character. Example: Use M*Entee to find McEntee and MacEntee and other variations. You could use M??Entee but you will only get results for two characters between M and Entee.

365. **Switch middle and first name.** Even if you are "certain" about an ancestor's name, be open to search variations. Swap the first and middle names. For some Catholic ancestors, the "confirmation" name was often adopted as a first name starting about age 13.

366. **Online genealogy records databases can disappear or be inaccessible!** Don't forget that most record sets on Ancestry and other sites are "licensed" by the repository and access is granted to users of the website. Licenses expire over time, and you may not realize it.

367. **Are you in the right time period?** The default search for Ancestry is to use the EXACT feature for names, dates, and locations. Remember to search "broad" first then drill down to more specific searching.

368. **Watch county boundaries!** Many states added or removed counties once added to the Union. You might think you are searching in the right county, but always check to see if that county actually existed for a specific date.

369. **OCR is NOT your friend.** Digitized historical newspapers can have an error rate as high as 20%. Review the record image; if the text interprets the letter "a" as "o," change your search criteria. Hyphens and diacritical marks can be problematic; again, review the record image and determine if adding these marks will improve the search.

370. **Spelling and phonetic substitutions.** Many records were created by an official based on what he was told. Many had difficulty understanding foreign languages and how names were written. Substitute different spellings during search attempts as well as different phonetic versions.

371. **Beware address and street name changes.** If you can't find information related to a specific address or street, keep in mind many locales changed street names over time OR instituted a new street numbering grid (like Chicago did in 1909!)

372. **Check the period jargon.** Abbreviated names were used to save space. Example: Thos. for Thomas and M'Entee for MacEntee. The terms our ancestors used for occupations and medical conditions might be different than present-day terminology.

Smarter Searching Resources

373. *A Beginner's Guide to Searching Records* – **FamilySearch**
https://www.familysearch.org/blog/en/a-beginners-guide-to-searching-records/

374. **Ancestry Card Catalog**
https://www.ancestry.com/search/collections/catalog/

375. **ArchiveGrid**
https://researchworks.oclc.org/archivegrid/

376. **Atlas of Historical County Boundaries**
http://publications.newberry.org/ahcbp/

377. **FamilySearch Catalog**
https://www.familysearch.org/search/catalog

378. **Glossary of Medical Terms Used in the 18th and 19th Centuries**
https://www.thornber.net/medicine/html/medgloss.html

379. **Google Alerts**
https://www.google.com/alerts

380. *How to Search Ancestry* – **Ancestry**
https://support.ancestry.com/s/article/How-to-Search-Ancestry

381. **List of Occupation Abbreviations – GenealogyInTime Magazine**
http://www.genealogyintime.com/dictionary/list-of-occupation-abbreviations-page-a.html

382. **MyHeritage Collection Catalog**
https://www.myheritage.com/research/catalog

383. *Record Search Tips: Find Your Family* – **FamilySearch**
https://www.familysearch.org/blog/en/record-search-tips/

384. **Spelling Substitution Tables for the United States and Canada – Family Search**
https://www.familysearch.org/wiki/en/Spelling_Substitution_Tables_for_the_United_States_and_Canada

385. **Street Name Changes**
http://stevemorse.org/census/changes.html

386. *What War Did My Ancestor Serve In?* - **Ancestry**
https://blogs.ancestry.com/ancestry/2014/04/23/what-war-did-my-ancestor-serve-in/

Social Media

Social media is a term that more and more genealogists and family historians encounter each day. Besides hearing or seeing Facebook and Twitter in the media, if you use the Internet as part of your research efforts, you most likely have already come across these programs and others. Social networking may appear to many of us to be all "fun and games" or "kid's stuff" or "a passing fad." Yet more business and organizations are leveraging it as part of their marketing and interaction with their customer base. Used wisely, social networking has great value for the genealogy community.

387. **Create your own blog**. A blog has been called "cousin bait for genealogists," meaning it is a way to get your research noticed especially by search engines. **Blogger** (https://www.blogger.com/) and **WordPress** (https://wordpress.com/) are the most popular blogging platforms.

388. **Join Facebook**. Check out the Facebook section of this book to set up an account, learn how to protect your privacy and more.

389. **Get on Twitter**. Sign up for **Twitter** (https://twitter.com/) and create a profile. Remember there is a 140-character limit for messages. Use the #genealogy hashtag and search for tweets at https://twitter.com/hashtag/genealogy.

Benefits of Social Networking for Genealogists

390. **Find other researchers working on the same surname or ancestral lines**. Many genealogists have stories to tell of how they have met long forgotten or even unknown family members on sites like Facebook. Currently researchers are using Twitter to see who else might be researching specific surnames, family lines or even subject matters such as DNA genealogy.

391. **Locate new resources for research**. Let's face it, there is no way any of us can track every new genealogy database, website, or blog. By following genealogy-focused people in social networking, you will get the latest news and resources.

392. **Get opinions and recommendations from other genealogists**. Once you build a community online, it is easier to get recommendations on genealogy database software or on how to write a difficult source citation.

393. **Publicize events and conferences for your genealogical society**. Groups are realizing how easy it is to connect with other genealogists and "get the word out" on upcoming happenings but also to drive traffic to their sites.

394. **Market your services or your genealogy-related company**. Social networking is a low-cost method of making sure a target audience learns about your services as a genealogist or products your genealogy-related company offers.

The Do's and Don'ts of Social Networking

As with any site, social networking is a world of "user beware" and here are some tips on how to protect yourself, your computer and your data while still enjoying the benefits of interacting with others.

395. **Only use sites that are permission-based**. This means sites where you need to allow people to follow you or see your content/information.

396. **Limit the amount of personal information you display both publicly and to friends/followers**. Do not include birth year, mother's maiden name, hometown and other items of information used to verify personal identity.

397. **Read and understand the Terms of Service agreement at all social networking sites**. It is your duty before signing up and using a service to know how your information will or will not be used by that site.

398. **Do not use email links to add friends/followers or to add applications**. This is a common way to pick up a computer virus. Go to the original site and you should use the notification there to add friends and content.

399. **It isn't all about you!** This means you need to listen, comment on the content of others, share information.

400. **Don't spam, don't oversell, or over-promote**. Social networking folks are very savvy and know when they smell bologna and cheese.

401. **Don't overload**. Don't share everything you find, don't feel the need to comment on every photo or item shared.

402. Don't race to build followers. Many new users of social networking think they need tons of followers right away. Focus on quality followers who share the same interests. Don't follow everyone that follows you – check out someone before following and make sure they are a "good fit."

403. Be human, be you. This is the most important part of social networking. People want to know there is a real person behind what is being published and shared.

Staying Safe Online

404. **Formula for Staying Safe**. The formula for a successful online experience involves these basic components: **Education** + **Action** + **Vigilance**.

- **Education**: Before you begin using any website, especially social media sites, make sure you fully understand how the site works.

- **Action**: Once you have signed up, work "smart" when using certain functions and check your settings!

- **Vigilance**: Don't become complacent . . . be vigilant when it comes to using social media!

405. **FREE Genealogy Books – Read the Fine Print and Don't Get Duped!** Beware of what appears to be a "free book scam" that I am seeing more and more each day as I read my Google Alerts. One of the alerts is for the term "genealogy" and believe me, Google Alerts seems to find anything and everything. What I am

finding are posts for genealogy and history book titles such as "Genealogical and Family History of Central New York."

Always Try Google Books BEFORE You Download!
If I had followed my instincts, I should have gone to Google Books and entered the title in the search field.

Terms of Service and Settings

406. Read and understand the Terms of Service. It is your duty before signing up and using a service to know how your information will or will not be used by that site. Don't click that "I accept the terms and conditions . . ." box until you have read the terms completely. Download and print out a copy if necessary.

407. Understand the privacy settings. Make sure you understand which personal information is publicly displayed on the website and how you can control the display of information. Download and print out a copy of the site's privacy policy. <u>Do not automatically accept the defaults provided by the site</u>. When in doubt, consult the Help section of the site.

408. Marketing and advertising information. Will the site gather information on your activity to feed you advertising or to advertise to your friends and followers on the site? It really depends on the site, but it is still your responsibility to know. Once you add an application, on Facebook for example, immediately go to Privacy Settings and see what data the app is collecting. Very often, you can change the settings to block some or all of the collecting features. Alternatively, simply remove the application if you do not feel comfortable with the collecting arrangement. Review the site's policies and learn how to change any marketing settings.

409. Stay up to date on policy changes. This means reading the e-mails about updates to a site's terms of service or privacy policy. Some sites have forums or RSS feeds where you can subscribe and get alerts. Again, you need to stay in the loop on what a social media site is doing with your information.

410. Removal of Information. What happens to your information if you decide to leave the site? Can you export your data? Do you have an exit strategy? Does the site retain any of your information once you have left?

Privacy

411. Limit the amount of personal information you display. This means information you display publicly and to friends or followers. Do not include your full birth date, hometown and other items of information used to verify personal identity. Remember: once information is posted, even though you change the display of that information later on, someone may have seen (and copied) the original data.

412. What does your employer see about you on social media? More and more employers are doing research about their employees on social media, and they do not always like what they find. Make sure you do not share information publicly <u>and</u> make sure you know who you allow to see your personal information.

413. Be anonymous if you want. This is not always easy to do but no one said you have to use your real name. Some sites like Facebook do not allow fake names and will either shut down your account or convert it to a Facebook page. Still, you might consider adopting an alias for social media accounts.

414. Is your birth date public? Facebook requires you to enter your birth year when signing up (to verify that you are over 13 years of age to meet their terms of service requirements) but make sure you go to Privacy settings and set the display settings to not show your birth year or just remove your birth date display.

415. Never give out your e-mail password, even to a social media site. Facebook and others try to convince you to find all your friends via your e-mail address book. Sounds like fun, right? Not if that site later uses your contacts to send advertising e-mails etc.

416. Do not post your daily routine. Again, just like location-based check-ins, do not let strangers know your daily habits such as walking to work, etc.

Friends and Followers

417. Use sites that are permission-based. This means a site where you give permission for people to follow you or see your content/information. With Facebook, you can grant permission before another user becomes your friend and has access to your information. Twitter, on the other hand, allows anyone to follow you with no permission needed. You can, however, block someone on Twitter once they have tried to follow you.

418. Do you really know your friend's friends? Remember what Mom used to say about knowing your friends' friends? Do you really know them? The same is true with social media. Avoid privacy settings that allow anyone who is not your friend to see your information or to even comment on status updates and photos.

419. **Mutual friends matter**. When receiving a friend request on Facebook, do you have mutual friends? If so, it is likely that the person is legit. Ask the person how they know you and why they want to interact with you on the site.

420. **Challenge and request more information**. When you receive a friend request from someone you do not know, send them a message, and ask how they know you and why they want to "friend" you. If you only use Facebook or other sites for genealogy, make it clear to the potential friend how you use the site and what information you are willing to exchange.

421. **Don't race to build followers**. Sure and steady wins the race, as they say. Who said you had to have 5,000 followers right away? Almost all e-mails offering to increase your followers are scams and they only want your login credentials to that social media site. Besides, what would you really do with 5,000 followers?

422. **Hide or unfriend**? On sites like Facebook, you can specify what types of updates you want to receive from someone. This means you can still be friends, but you want to narrow the information you see about them.

423. **Unfriend when needed**. Have no qualms about pruning your friends or followers list especially if a person does not respect your privacy or shares information about you inappropriately.

Games and Applications

424. Games can be misleading. Do you really know what you are getting into when you agree to download a game app on Facebook or another social media site? Again, read the Terms of Service. Many games seem like fun, but they are collecting data on what you click on within Facebook or another site and some games even follow what else you do on your computer or on the Internet.

425. Understand how 3rd party applications work. A site may ask you to authorize using it with another site via an application so that when you post content to one site it may appear on your Facebook page etc. Take time to read the Terms of Service for that application as well as how it will be using your content!

426. Avoid quizzes! You may be asked to answer "20 simple things about me" or another type of quiz. They seem like fun don't they? You answer questions about yourself and share it with friends on social media. However, have you ever looked closely at what type of data is being collected? Birthplace, birthday, school info . . . all items that can be used to steal your identity. Avoid quizzes and do not perpetuate them by sharing with others.

Pitfalls and Stuff to Avoid

427. Avoid e-mail links to add friends/followers or to add applications. You will probably receive a "confirmation" email once you sign up for a social media site; <u>it is fine to click the link on these emails</u>. However, you may get subsequent email notifications about new friends or people who wanted to connect with you.

Be very careful with these emails especially since spammers can create emails that look like they are from Facebook and these other sites! The basic rule is this: if the notification is true, then you should receive a notice at the original site as well.

This means you should delete the email, sign in to the site, and then check your notifications there. Never sign in to a site using a link in an email. This is how your account at the site can be hacked and compromised!

428. **Do not accept offers to build followers**. You may also receive emails or messages with offers from services that can help you get more friends and followers. Don't take the bait! Most of these services are scams that simply want access to your account in order to spam others. Build your friends and followers by adding them yourself or waiting to be invited by others.

429. **Be careful with location services.** Location services are a hot ticket these days with many folks stating where they are and who they are with, but who is watching the house or minding the store? Do not advertise your activities publicly, especially concerning vacations and the like.

430. **Beware of shortened URLs**. With the increasing popularity of social media, spammers have taken advantage of the increased use of shortened URLs to hide their links. Use a program that can reveal the true web address of a shortened URL like **ExpandURL** (https://www.expandurl.net/) or use an aggregation program like **Hootsuite** (https://www.hootsuite.com/) which expand shortened URLS.

Take Action

431. **Block and report spam posts and spammers.** Most sites have mechanisms to mark an update as spam or in violation of the site's Terms of Service. In addition, report specific users if they violate the rules of the site.

432. **Learn to post privately.** This means knowing the difference between a public post and a private post. In addition, do not forget that when you post publicly, on Facebook for example, **it will remember the last setting!** Always check the setting before posting and change back to private when needed.

433. **Use a "burn" e-mail address.** Set up a dummy e-mail account that you only use with social media. Forward the account to your real e-mail account.

434. **Use strong passwords.** Take time to construct a password that is easy for you to remember but not for a hacker to guess at. Avoid names of family members, locations etc. Use combinations of letters, numbers, and special characters.

435. **Fake your security information.** When asked for security information, either use fake data or provide information that others would not know about you. Example: for mother's maiden name, who said it has to actually be your mother's maiden name? Be consistent with usage across all social media sites.

436. **Install a good antivirus and spyware protection program on your computer.** You do not need to spend a lot and some programs are even available for free! A good program (for free) is **Avast** (https://www.avast.com).

Tech Grab Bag

437. **Future Proofing Your Technology**. "Future proofing" means not allowing technology to become outdated, especially technology where your genealogy data is stored. This means migrating from 3 1/2" floppy discs to the cloud or moving to a new version of the Windows operating system (example: WindowsXP is no longer supported). Don't be caught up in a situation where you rely upon third-party vendors to convert data for you!

438. **Trade In Your Gadgets**. Are you sitting on outdated technology such as an old smartphone? First, contact your cell provider to see if you are due for a free phone upgrade. Next, check out sites like **Gazelle** (https://www.gazelle.com/) that accept old phones and other equipment in exchange for Amazon gift cards or cash. Moreover, do not forget that the **Amazon Trade In Program** (https://genealogybargains.com/amazon-tradeinprogram) will accept books, phones and video games.

439. URL Shorteners. Use a URL shortener to make a long link to a website easier to remember or create a "vanity URL" with your name or the name of your genealogy society. Popular shorteners include **bit.ly** (https://bitly.com/) and **TinyURL** (https://tinyurl.com/). Also, beware of shortened URLs sent to you from unfamiliar sources. Use a site like **ExpandURL** (https://www.expandurl.net/) to decipher the underlying link and source for a shortened URL.

440. Visit the Internet Archive. Internet Archive (https://archive.org/) is a site with over 1 million digitized texts and books including Federal and state census books. Always look on Internet Archive for a book before making a purchase! Bonus: use **The Wayback Machine** to view those web pages that no longer exist.

441. Web Browser Extensions. Most web browsers, including Firefox, Google Chrome and Internet Explorer have access to a library of "helper apps." These browser extensions can translate foreign language text, take notes and more. See *Web Browser Extensions: Power Up Your Genealogy* (https://www.archives.com/experts/macentee-thomas/web-browser-extensions-power-up-your-genealogy.html) .

442. Take advantage of Wolfram Alpha tools. Need to know the weather for a specific date? What about calculating a birth date based on a death date from a gravestone? **Wolfram Alpha** (https://www.wolframalpha.com/) is a computational knowledgebase that accesses over 10,000 databases to return information based on specified sets of calculation requests. Example: enter **grandmother's aunt** at Wolfram Alpha and a family tree will appear along with other data including a blood fraction percentage.

443. **Get answers to genealogy tech questions**. Join the **Technology for Genealogy** group on Facebook (https://www.facebook.com/groups/techgen/) and then either post your find or post a query and ask for help in understanding the tool.

444. **Most states have resident-only research websites**. It is true. Most states have a website that can be accessed from home if you have a public library card. One example is **BadgerLink** (https://badgerlink.dpi.wi.gov/) which allows Wisconsin residents access to historical newspapers and more.

Travel Tips

Genealogists love to travel, whether it is in search of new records, traipsing through cemeteries, or wandering around an ancestral homeland.

A Genealogist's Packing List

445. Whether you are going on a research trip, traveling to a genealogy conference, or attending a family reunion, be prepared for any and every genealogy encounter! Review ***A Genealogists' Packing List*** (https://genealogybargains.com/cs-genrestrip) for ideas . . . better yet, print it out and use it as a checklist!

How to Handle Emergencies

Once you have planned and packed, the next step is making the trip. Remember that there is only so much you can worry about and control once you are on your way. If you can recognize what you can and cannot do in situations, your memories of any trip – even one where everything seemed to go "not as planned" – will be cherished forever.

446. **Weather**. Stay on top of weather developments using websites and mobile apps on your smartphone. Also, have contingency plans for those segments of your trip that involve outside work, such as visiting a cemetery. You may need to be flexible and swap your cemetery day with a library research day.

447. **Air Travel**. If you have not traveled by air in the past three to five years, you are in for a surprise since flying requires patience. Visit the ***Transportation Security Administration*** (https://www.tsa.gov) website at and understand the procedures for getting through security and what you can and can't bring onboard.

448. **Train Travel**. While going by train can be fun and relaxing, realize that at least here in the United States, freight companies that have the right of way often own rail lines. Do not count on being on time and allow yourself an extra hour or two to get to your destination.

449. **Car Travel**. Driving requires you to be at your best at all times; this means wide-awake and with eyes on the road. Avoid distractions and make sure you take breaks if needed. Get plenty of rest the night before and do not drive if you are sleepy or impaired. Also, schedule the car for a tune up before any long trip!

450. **Call Home**. If you travel solo, check in with a friend or a family member once you arrive at your destination and then on a daily basis. If you are stuck for any reason – weather, car repair, etc. – reach out to your network of friends and fellow researchers via social media. They might be able to steer you towards places to stay, eat, or even put you up for the night in an emergency.

451. Health Emergencies. Make sure you have all your medications; better yet, take photos on your smartphone of each prescription bottle and information in case you lose them. Use your research skills to find the closest urgent care facility or 24-hour pharmacy. Notify family members if you fall ill and ask for their help.

Leverage Loyalty Programs

452. Points and perks: Take advantage of loyalty programs which award points and perks even if you are not a frequent traveler. Make sure you are signed in with your account information <u>before</u> booking a reservation. When checking in at a hotel or picking up a car, make sure they have noted your loyalty account number. In addition, use points to get free rooms and free air tickets or upgrades.

Sponsored Research Trips

453. Many societies offer organized trips to key locations relevant to genealogy research. These include American cities such as Salt Lake City, Utah, home of the Family History Library or Fort Wayne, Indiana, where the Allen County Public Library is located. These trips focus solely on research and access to libraries and repositories. You will sometimes find classes by well-known genealogy speakers and research consultants who will assist you in accessing the resources you need.

Set Up Alerts for Deals and Discounts

Here are some tips on how to stay on top of available deals when it comes to travel. Remember that the more you save, the more you can spend on the "extras."

454. Timing: If you are planning way in advance, learn the best time of year to make the trip to specific destinations. Either visit during off times when most tourists are absent or the "shoulder season" which is a month or two before and after the prime travel period. Also be flexible when searching for airfares; many sites will display the fares several days before and after your desired departure date.

455. Collect information: Keep a binder or a digital folder where you can stuff items you locate during the year related to your trip. This includes coupons, special events, and information on places to visit.

456. Get notified: Sign up for sale notifications at various websites. Include your preferred airlines, hotels and other travel vendors.

Travel Apps and Websites

457. Planning. Looking for an upcoming genealogy event with a nearby research location? **Conference Keepers** (https://www.conferencekeeper.org) lists genealogy conferences and events all over the world. Ever wonder if it is better to fly or drive to your next genealogy-related location? **TravelMath** (https://www.travelmath.com) has you covered. Looking to share a ride?

458. Air Travel. Check out **Kayak** (https://www.kayak.com) and **skyscanner** (https://www.skyscanner.com) to look for the best airfares. Also, download the app for your preferred airline before you travel to stay on top of delays and cancellations or to use a virtual boarding pass.

459. Train Travel. **Amtrak** has its own app (https://www.amtrak.com) to book travel.

460. Car Travel. Looking for cheap gas? Check out **Gas Buddy** (https://gasbuddy.com) which helps you find the best priced fuel near your location. **Waze** (https://www.waze.com) is a reliable navigation program good for car travel.

461. Travel Emergencies. Make sure you have the tools to survive any emergency on your trip. Use **mPassport** (https://www.mpassport.com/index.cfm) to communicate with others to get help.

462. Stay In Touch. Make sure you take advantage of the mobile version of **Skype** (https://www.skype.com) if you have a Skype account.

463. Food. Look to **Yelp** (https://www.yelp.com) to locate a restaurant nearby, complete with directions. Stuck at a place that does not have room service? Order take-out or get it delivered using **GrubHub** (https://www.grubhub.com) . . . you can even pay using Paypal! If you are fan of the unusual eateries then check out **Roadfood** (https://www.roadfood.com) for those diners and dives!

464. Accommodation. Many use **TripAdvisor** (https://www.tripadvisor.com) to get recommended hotels and other places to stay; do not forget to leave your own review for the places you've stayed. **Hotel Tonight** (https://www.hoteltonight.com) comes to the rescue if your original reservation is cancelled or the accommodations are not to your liking.

465. Get Your Geek On. Looking for the closest Wi-Fi? Try **Wi-Fi Map** (https://www.wifimap.io).

466. Fun Stuff. **Roadtrippers** (https://roadtrippers.com) can help you find unusual roadside attractions. **Madlibs** (https://www.madlibs.com) is now available as a mobile app and can keep your entire entourage entertained on a long trip. For entertainment events, go to **TimeOut** (https://www.timeout.com) and find what is going on in a destination city.

Time To Go Pro?

Many genealogists and family historians will at some point consider "turning pro," a term that could mean taking on paying research clients or proving genealogical research competency via certification and accreditation.

467. Board for Certification of Genealogists. Visit the **BCG** website (https://bcgcertification.org/) not only to learn more about certification but for their excellent educational resources.

468. ProGen Study Groups. At **ProGen** (https://progenstudygroups.com/) professional and aspiring genealogists commit to an 18-month collaborative journey review of the book **Professional Genealogy: Preparation, Practice & Standards** (https://genealogybargains.com/amazon-progen).

469. **International Commission for the Accreditation of Professional Genealogists**. **ICAPGEN** (https://www.icapgen.org/) offers accreditation of genealogists in various subject matters within the genealogy industry. In addition, their website offers excellent educational resources.

470. **Association of Professional Genealogists**. A professional association for genealogy professionals, **APG** (https://www.apgen.org/) is a membership organization offering resources and discounts to members.

Starting a Genealogy Business

Have you thought seriously about starting your own genealogy and family history –related business? Have you researched our own genealogy and also done so for friends who've said, "You should do this for a living?" Do you think that researching your own ancestors is "fun" and that it would make a good way to earn a living?

The truth is that establishing any business is more difficult than you think. Only 50% of new small businesses survive past the five-year mark, only 33% do so for ten years or more. Realize there is no "easy button" in creating and running a genealogy business; just like any other business you need to deal with planning, marketing, taxes, legal issues and more besides the actual "client work." You'll put in way more than "40 hours a week" and you'll nurture your new enterprise just like a child. But the rewards are many and the chance to direct your own work choices and income earning potential.

Set Goals and Create a Business Plan

471. **Envision your ideal genealogy business.** What would the name of the business be? What type of product or service would you provide? How much income would you earn the first year? How much time would you work in the first year? Write a one paragraph statement that accurately describes your new business.

472. **Create a list of goals.** Be practical and write down a bullet-point list of goals along with a time frame for each goal. Cover products and services, number of customers, work location, etc.

473. **Build your business plan.** Use some of the standard business plan template available through the **Small Business Administration** (https://www.sba.gov/) or online and create a business plan.

Read, Write and THINK

Before and during that time when the great idea of having a genealogy business has entered your head, commit yourself to doing lots of reading, writing, and thinking. This will help you narrow your focus, set realistic goals, and create a solid and sustainable business plan.

474. **Read** business blogs and magazines as well as the blogs run by other genealogy business owners, especially those you admire and respect.

475. **Write** about a product or service currently available in the genealogy business and consider how you'd offer a better version or something similar.

476. **Think** about what it would take to make that product or service a reality.

Finances and Taxes

While you may be able to start a business on a shoestring budget, there are some costs that can't be negotiated such as licenses and permits, marketing expenses, office space and supplies. You'll need to decide which approach to take:

477. **Self-financing.** If you are sitting on cash or convertible assets, you can use those to start your business. If you decide to cash in retirement savings such as an IRA, understand there may be tax penalties and issues.

478. **Loans.** A better way of accumulating startup capital might be the use of loans through the Small Business Loan program or even to take a loan against an IRA, rather than a direct disbursement. There are also special loans for minority and women-owned businesses.

479. **Grants.** Check your county and state resources under "small business" or "business administration" to see if there are grants available.

480. **Investors.** In these days of crowdfunding sites like Kickstarter, you may be tempted to bring on investors. Realize that for each investment, that percentage, be it 5%, 10% or more, is the amount of "control" you relinquish. Choose your investment vehicles and your investors carefully.

481. **Bookkeeping and tracking income/expenses.** How will you track expenses and incoming revenue? Consider using programs such as QuickBooks which make it easy for first time business owners.

Legal Issues

In each state and even local city or township, you may be required to file paperwork to establish a business, even if you opt to set up a "sole proprietorship."

482. What type of business? There are many choices including Sole Proprietorship, C Corporation, Limited Liability Corporation and more. Each business type has its own filing requirements, usually with your state's Secretary of State or Corporations office.

483. Licenses and permits. Check to make sure you have all operating permits and licenses on a state and local level.

484. Seek legal counsel. Check with your local chamber of commerce or online at the county or state level for free legal resources. Some venues offer drop-in legal clinics or can connect you with law firms that might provide basic services.

Marketing

485. Join The Genealogists Marketing Sourcebook on Facebook. Share tips and get advice from fellow genealogy entrepreneurs at **Genealogists Marketing Sourcebook** (https://www.facebook.com/groups/genealogistsmarketing/) on Facebook.

Networking and Professional Development

486. Network online and in-person. Especially when running a business from a home office, it is easy to become isolated from others in your field. Make sure that you are networking both online and in-person at genealogy events. Use **LinkedIn** (https://www.linkedin.com/) and build your niche by listing your skills, sharing genealogy-related news items, and connecting with leaders in the field.

487. Business cards still work! At genealogy conferences and events make sure you have a business card available to hand out at lectures and in the exhibit hall. Make it a point to visit vendors and discuss their products so they'll remember you at the next event.

Marketing and Selling

488. Create a Web presence. Besides business cards mentioned above, you'll need to have a web presence for your new business. **Weebly** (https://www.weebly.com/) is a free website creation tool with easy-to-use templates. A good business website should cover the basics including a bio, a list of products and services, and contact information.

Analytics

489. How's business? Once your business is launched, keep checking your business plan and adjust periodically. Check and see which products and services are selling and which ones are not. Remember to try new things which includes using different social media platforms for marketing.

The Future of Genealogy

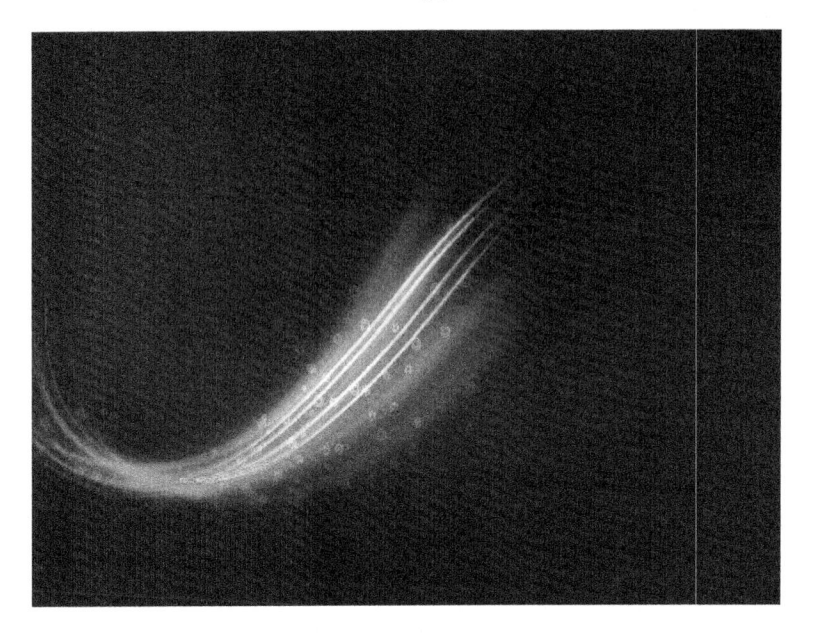

490. Big Data becomes the backbone of online genealogy. When it comes down to it, the major vendors in genealogy space are really just "big data" companies. Ancestry.com's main asset is its collection of over 30 billion records. When you think about it, Ancestry and other companies take two approaches to monetizing their records: 1) they provide ways to "easily" search the records and find your ancestors; and 2) they "gamify" the process of doing genealogy by letting you build family trees, connect with other researchers, share information with family members etc. This "gamification" is key because much of it represents work performed by members and users which is then uploaded and incorporated into Ancestry's growing database.

So look for new ways to work with data which could mean: reindexing of data sets including new fields added to the original index (occupation added to a US Census which was not part of the original index);

advanced story telling such as how Ancestry is using **Story Scout** (https://genealogybargains.com/ancestry-storyscout) to bring many different data points together so users can get a better idea of an ancestor's life; and the use of "pinning" either to maps/geography programs or to story board similar to Pinterest despite concerns about copyright and how vendors can control any "leakage" of records out to sites like Pinterest.

491. **Crowdsourcing of genealogy record sets continues.** Given the success of the **1940 US Census** indexing (https://www.archives.gov/research/census/1940/faqs), completed in 123 days, look for more projects requiring volunteer indexers. While **FamilySearch Indexing** (https://www.familysearch.org/getinvolved/) continues with volunteers on existing projects, look for individuals to start their own crowd-sourced projects as well as genealogy societies indexing their own holdings.

492. **DNA testing results will provide breakthroughs for many.** Look for continued growth in the area of DNA testing for ancestry and genealogy purposes. The use of DNA testing by genealogists and family historians will continue to grow. In addition, DNA testing will be one of the key "hooks" to bring newcomers into the genealogy and family history market.

    Look for these advances in the area of DNA: more webinars and educational materials to understand DNA results, better and easier ways to connect with other testers to share results and share research, more tools to facilitate such connections and improve data interpretations.

493. **Genealogy education moves beyond the lecture format.** Genealogy education will continue to evolve and branch out beyond the typical 50-minute lecture with 10 minutes of Q&A, whether it is in-person or

online. Look at the growth of in-person institutes such as **Genealogical Research Institute of Pittsburgh** and **Salt Lake Institute of Technology** where tracks and sessions are focused on specific ethnicities, record sets. Many of these in-person venues also offer collaborative project participation and problem solving; these techniques will next migrate to the online genealogy sphere. In addition, it appears that genealogists finally understand that good genealogy education has value and therefore an admission fee must be charged.

494. **Heritage travel sees moderate growth increase**. As more Baby Boomers retire, they will want to visit the places where their grandparents, great-grandparents and other ancestors lived. This includes those with little or no research experience. Heritage travel will cater to both the casual family historian as well as the serious genealogist seeking research assistance at local archives and repositories.

495. **Life streaming is embraced by genealogists as well as the general public**. One thing that we as genealogists don't do is document our own lives and experiences. Perhaps because we are so focused on documenting the lives of our ancestors, we suffer from the "cobbler's children have no shoes" syndrome.

    There are many apps and programs available under the category of "life streaming" and some would say that **Facebook**, **Twitter**, and other social media platforms can serve this purpose of assembling a personal diary. But the keyword is "personal" since many of these sites are very public.

    One twist you could see: having these apps used to develop an ancestor diary. Already there are "historical Twitter accounts" that actually tweet diaries of the famous and not so famous. It isn't so far-fetched to think that genealogists sitting on a collection of ancestor diary materials might take to these platforms to share information about their ancestors. Also, look for more and more methods of keeping a personal journal and more genealogists using these tools for their own life streaming projects.

496. **Life Consolidation continues to be an unpleasant but necessary task; opportunities for entrepreneurs abound.** This is a difficult topic for which there isn't, nor should there be, a catchy title: **how do you handle cleaning out the home of a parent or loved one after they die, or they are placed in a care facility**? Having been through this journey myself, I struggle with the terminology. "Boxing up a life" seems so cold but there is that aspect to the process.

    Especially as Baby Boomers begin dealing with this process, they also come to the realization that someone will have to do the same for them in 20 or 30 or more years. Any technology that can simplify the "tracking of items" or assist with organizing and scanning documents and images will be more and more attractive to everyone, not just family historians. This is a growing niche and its own industry – how to settle an estate, disperse family mementos yet also celebrate a person's life through storytelling. Look for specific apps and platforms geared towards this problem and providing solutions.

497. **Newcomers discover genealogy through various media channels.** A trend started with the BBC television show ***Who Do You Think You Are?*** (https://www.bbc.co.uk/programmes/b007t575) will continue across different media channels including television, radio, online videos and more. The merger of reality television with genealogy and family history will increase, already evident in shows such as ***Genealogy Roadshow*** on **PBS**

(https://www.pbs.org/show/genealogy-roadshow/) in the United State and ***Allt för Sverige*** (https://www.svtplay.se/allt-for-sverige) in Sweden.

498. **Privacy fears will not disappear and may hamper genealogy industry growth**. Protecting one's privacy became an even bigger challenge given the revelations about the NSA and metadata / phone surveillance here in the United States. One emerging trend in 2015 will be the creation of "personal clouds" which are self-hosted. This means instead of placing your data on **Dropbox** and accessing it from various devices, you will create your own cloud site and make it private.

499. **Storytelling brings in new users to genealogy**. And once you've gathered research and information on a loved one or an ancestor, how do you make sure it is preserved and shared with others? There are so many choices for storytelling out in the marketplace that most are overwhelmed. One thing you'll see develop are Facebook groups and educational offerings to assist users in telling the best story possible. Both video and audio will be popular and highly shareable with family members.

500. **Tablets and mobile devices will continue to increase in popularity**. More and more users will be purchasing tablet type devices meaning tablet computers and multi-purpose devices such as the Kindle Fire or the Samsung Galaxy. There is a trend towards "2 in 1" devices such as tablets that convert to a laptop etc. Genealogists are starting to use these devices for "portable research" meaning they can have a virtual research assistant readily available especially when they visit an archive or repository.

    Of course, not every repository will allow such devices – remember to call ahead and ask (do not rely on websites which might not be updated). Genealogists don't want to be tied down to a computer at the archive – they want to use their device which might be loaded with apps like their genealogy database software, their files, scanned documents, photos etc.

In addition, genealogists are using these tablet-type devices to do more and more scanning or capturing of documents. Applications like **Reimagine** (https://genealogybargains.com/reimagine) make this possible.

About the Author – Thomas MacEntee

So, what if I told you that a Baby Boomer guy with a love of punk rock music but also Renaissance Art, somehow "fell" into the technology industry almost 40 years ago, and then left a lucrative career in information technology to pursue his love of family history and genealogy?

And that his passion for tracing his roots began over 45 years ago when he was watching the mini-series Roots on ABC Television at his great-grandparents' house in February 1977?

While some might think these two elements - technology and historical research – are opposites. The truth is, "tech people" like Thomas are needed to guide today's genealogists through the maze of options so they can deploy the best apps and devices as they break down those research brick walls.

Having taught over 1,000 in-person and virtual genealogy lectures since 2010, serving on the boards of many genealogical societies, organizing a group of over 1,000 genealogy bloggers, and helping researchers save money on genealogy products and services, Thomas is ready for the next chapter in his professional journey: changing the way genealogists acquire new research skills, motivating researchers to take a chance on new technologies, and improving how family stories and heirlooms are preserved and passed on to the next generations.

Thomas MacEntee: author, educator, student, advocate, marketer, storyteller, entrepreneur, and that "genealogy guy" who helps you accomplish your family history goals.

Ways to Connect with Thomas MacEntee

Genealogy & Technology E-News
https://genealogybargains.com/enews
Stay up to date with the latest offers from Ancestry, Findmypast, MyHeritage and more! Includes my technology articles and "how to" tips and tricks for genealogists.

Genealogy Bargains
https://wwwgenealogybargains.com
Genealogy Bargains scours the Internet and works closely with many genealogy vendors to secure the best deals, the best coupons, and the best savings for you.

Facebook Group The Genealogy Do Over
https://www.facebook.com/groups/genealogydoover
The Genealogy Do-Over combines genealogy education on methodology and practice AS WELL AS recalling family memories to inspire genealogists to capture their own memories in a fixed form.

Facebook Group Thomas' Genealogy Tree House
https://www.facebook.com/groups/gentreehouse/
Thomas' Genealogy Tree House is your "club house" for family history "how to's" from genealogy expert and author Thomas MacEntee.

Facebook Page Genealogy Bargains
https://www.facebook.com/genealogybargains/

Twitter – Genealogy Bargains
https://twitter.com/geneabargains

Threads – Genealogy Bargains
https://www.threads.net/@genealogybargains

Instagram – Genealogy Bargains
https://www.instagram.com/genealogybargains/

Pinterest – Genealogy Bargains
https://www.pinterest.com/genealogybargains

FREE Genealogy Cheat Sheets

Download a variety of easy-to-use, free genealogy cheat sheets created by genealogy expert Thomas MacEntee of GenealogyBargains.com. Please SHARE these 2-sided cheat sheets with your genealogy friends and fellow genealogy society members!

Visit https://genealogybargains.com/free-genealogy-cheat-sheets/ for free access!

- 10 Cloud Computing Tips for Genealogy
- 10 Google Books Tips for Genealogy
- 10 Google Tools for Genealogy
- 10 Smarter Search Strategies for Genealogy
- 10 Things You Need To Know About Copyright & Genealogy

- 10 Tips & Tools for Transcribing Genealogy Documents
- 10 Tips & Tricks for Military Records and Genealogy
- 10 Tips for Outsourcing Your Family Photo Scanning
- 10 Tips for Successful US Census Research
- 10 Ways to Document Disasters in Genealogy Research
- 10 Ways to Save Money on Genealogy
- 10 Ways to Use Internet Archive for Genealogy
- 10 Ways to Use School Yearbooks for Genealogy
- 10 Ways to Use Wolfram Alpha for Genealogy
- 14 Tips to Speed Up Your Genealogy Computer
- 18 Ways to Get the Most from Family Member Interviews
- 20 Best Genealogy, DNA, and Family History Apps
- 20 Tips for Staying Safe Online
- 20 Ways to Play Nice in the Genealogy Sandbox
- 25 Tips for "Do It Yourself" Family Photo Scanning
- 40+ Transportation Resources for Genealogy
- 1950 US Census Research Tracking Sheet (Excel)
- Backing Up Your Genealogy Data
- Checklist for Preserving Family Oral History
- City Directories – 10 Tips & Tricks for Genealogy
- Creating a Mixtiles Family Tree
- Did I Get Everything - Genealogy Research Checklists
- Documenting Family Stories in Writing
- Excel Shortcut Keys
- Genealogy Research Log (Excel download)
- Genealogy Research Trip Packing List
- Historical Maps: 10 Tips & Tricks for Genealogy

- Historical Newspapers: 10 Tips & Tricks for Genealogy
- How Do I Know What I Don't Know in Genealogy?
- Research Strategies for Addresses and Genealogy
- Research Strategies for Names and Genealogy
- Research Strategies for Occupations and Genealogy
- Top 10 German Genealogy Resources
- Word Shortcut Keys
- You Use What? – 10 Apps & Tips for Genealogy